NATIONAL SECURITY RESEARCH DIVISION

Libya After Qaddafi

Lessons and Implications for the Future

Christopher S. Chivvis, Jeffrey Martini

Prepared for the Smith Richardson Foundation

The research described in this report was sponsored by the Smith Richardson Foundation and conducted within the International Security and Defense Policy Center of the RAND National Security Research Division.

Library of Congress Cataloging-in-Publication Data is available for this publication.

ISBN: 978-0-8330-8489-7

The RAND Corporation is a nonprofit institution that helps improve policy and decisionmaking through research and analysis. RAND's publications do not necessarily reflect the opinions of its research clients and sponsors.

Support RAND—make a tax-deductible charitable contribution at www.rand.org/giving/contribute.html

RAND® is a registered trademark

Cover image by Reuters/Amr Abdallah Dalsh

© Copyright 2014 RAND Corporation

RAND OFFICES

SANTA MONICA, CA • WASHINGTON, DC

PITTSBURGH, PA • NEW ORLEANS, LA • JACKSON, MS • BOSTON, MA

DOHA, QA • CAMBRIDGE, UK • BRUSSELS, BE

www.rand.org

Preface

This report assesses Libya's first two years after the fall of Muammar Qaddafi in 2011. It analyzes key developments in political, military, and economic areas, and explains the role of the international community. Drawing on existing literature on civil wars and post-conflict reconstruction, it outlines steps the international community might take to improve Libya's future outlook and draws some tentative conclusions about the implications of Libya's experience for future post-conflict reconstruction efforts. A particular focus is the consequences of the failure to establish security in the immediate aftermath of the war.

The situation in Libya is dynamic and continues to develop, as do the policies of Libya's international supporters who have been involved in helping Libya manage a very difficult transition from war to peace. The work was begun in 2012. This is the final report of the project, and takes into account developments through early 2014.

Funding was provided by the Smith Richardson Foundation. The research was conducted within the International Security and Defense Policy Center of the RAND National Security Research Division (NSRD). NSRD conducts research and analysis on defense and national security topics for the U.S. and allied defense, foreign policy, homeland security, and intelligence communities and foundations and other nongovernmental organizations that support defense and national security analysis.

For more information on the International Security and Defense Policy Center, see http://www.rand.org/nsrd/ndri/centers/isdp.html or contact the director (contact information is provided on the web page).

Contents

Figures

Summary

Since the 2011 overthrow of the Qaddafi regime, Libya's path has been tumultuous. Despite a number of advantages compared with other post-conflict societies, progress on political, economic, and security fronts has fallen far behind, generating frustration and threatening the recovery altogether. Libya has teetered on the brink of a relapse into civil war on more than one occasion in the past year. In the absence of a functioning state, jihadist groups have made inroads. The broader Sahel and Maghreb regions, meanwhile, are becoming more and more fragile and southern Libya verges on becoming a safe haven for al Qaeda–linked groups recently chased from Mali by French military forces.

The right international approach to Libya could nevertheless still help avert a more serious breakdown and real damage to U.S. and European regional and global interests—above all counterterrorism and the stability of world energy markets.

This study examines what has been accomplished in Libya to date, draws lessons from the experience, and identifies some possible ways forward.

Lack of Security

Libya's most serious problem since 2011 has been the lack of security. Insecurity has had negative repercussions across the spectrum. It has undermined efforts to build functioning political and administrative institutions, further constricted an already minimal international footprint, and facilitated the expansion of criminal and jihadist groups within Libya and the wider region. Libyan political leaders have been under constant threat of attack, as displayed most dramatically in the October 2013 kidnapping of Prime Minister Ali Zeidan.

The lack of security stems primarily from the failure of the effort to disarm and demobilize rebel militias after the war. Both international advisors and Libya's political leadership recognized the importance of rebel disarmament from the outset, but neither has been able to implement it. As a result, various types of armed groups control much of the country and the elected government is at their mercy. Until the security situation is brought under control, progress on all other fronts will be very slow and always at risk.

Stalled Statebuilding Process

The lack of security has greatly undermined an already difficult statebuilding process in Libya, where the post-Qaddafi state was very weak politically and administratively. To begin with, Libya's constitutional process has not kept pace with the schedule originally set out during the war. That schedule aimed to provide Libya with a constitution within a year of liberation. More than two years after Qaddafi's death, however, the constitutional drafting committee has yet to begin its work.

Meanwhile, groups in the eastern province of Cyrenaica have seized control of oil facilities there and threatened to create an autonomous state-within-a-state. Islamist and revolutionary groups have forced the passage of a political isolation law that excludes many Libyans from participation in government, thus exacerbating existing rifts in society and reducing the available pool of talent for government positions. The General National Congress, which was elected in July 2012, has been deeply divided over many issues.

In general, Libyan public administration is in very poor shape and capacity building is sorely needed to strengthen the state. Public confidence in the democratic political process has declined as frustration has mounted. In the absence of a national state, regional and tribal substate actors have strengthened and will likely seek to hold onto their entrenched power.

Economic Challenges

Oil production restarted quickly in the aftermath of the war and has allowed Libya to avoid some of the most serious choices that post-conflict societies face because it could fund reconstruction and pay salaries to many groups, including militias. With the armed takeover of many of Libya's oil facilities in the summer of 2013, however, the stability of Libya's economy—including the ability of the government to continue to pay salaries indefinitely—was drawn into question. Libya also eventually needs economic reforms that will create a more business-friendly environment. The postwar Libyan government has taken a few steps in the right direction, but it has also been forced to increase government salaries and subsidies, both of which distort the economy and work against sustainable, broad-based economic growth.

Upping the International Role

Despite a significant investment of military and political capital in helping the Libyan rebels overthrow Qaddafi, international actors have done very little to support Libya's post-conflict recovery to date. In contrast with all other cases of NATO military intervention, a very small United Nations (UN) mission with no executive authority has led the international effort to help stabilize the country. The United States and its NATO allies have played a very limited role.

International actors have recently started increasing their efforts in Libya somewhat. More should have been done and still needs to be done, however. The United States and its allies have both moral and strategic interests in ensuring that Libya does not collapse back into civil war or become a safe haven for al Qaeda or other jihadist groups within striking distance of Europe. Terrorist violence is already a problem in Libya, and any increase could have a devastating impact on the fragile and failing Sahel region. Needless to say, if Libya were to become a terrorist safe haven, it would be a very serious problem for the West and a tragic end to the West's well-intentioned and initially very effective effort to topple Qaddafi. It would be tragic if that initial victory were allowed to turn into strategic defeat.

In contrast, if Libya sees gradual political stabilization under representative government and constitutional rule, the United States and its allies would benefit from Libya's energy and other resources. The region as a whole would also be much stronger.

Improvements will take time, but despite its current challenges, Libya still has many advantages when compared with other post-conflict societies. Notably, it can foot much of the bill for its post-conflict needs—even if it currently lacks the administrative capacity to manage complex payments to foreign entities.

The Way Forward

Improving Libya's future prospects will take several years, given the limited international role. There are four areas that international actors should focus on while looking ahead:

Support a National Reconciliation Process

The most serious problem in Libya today is continued insecurity, which impedes political and other advances and could wipe them out altogether. Absent an international peacekeeping force, which should be considered but would be difficult under current circumstances, the best way to improve security is to engage Libyans in a national reconciliation dialogue. Such a process could facilitate disarmament, complement constitution making, and increase international actors' access to information about the capabilities and intentions of key Libyan groups. Although the process would need strong support from the Libyan government itself, outside actors, such as the UN or European Union (EU), could play crucial facilitating and mediating roles. Objectives of such a process could include creating a vehicle for broader discussions of disarmament, establishing rules of the road, and generally building trust and increasing the flow of information between different Libyan groups. Ideally, the process would be led by a high-level European, such as Paddy Ashdown, or another figure of international stature from a Muslim country. The newly created position of U.S. Special Coordinator for Libya could also play a role.

Strengthen Libya's National Security Forces

Insecurity in Libya is partially attributable to a lack of reliable national security forces. International actors are well placed to help remedy this lacuna, and Libya is prepared to foot the bill. Recent U.S. and European efforts to train a so-called "general-purpose force" of approximately 15,000 over the next several years will help. The effort should proceed in parallel with reconciliation and strike a balanced representation of Libyan society, lest individual groups perceive the training as being directed against them and revolt. Police training is also much needed.

These efforts need to be fully funded. The Libyans should pay for as much as possible, but other countries should also contribute as needed, especially while Libya's institutional capacity for payments is still weak.

Help Libya Strengthen Border Security

Border security remains a major challenge. The porousness of Libya's borders and their susceptibility to smuggling and the circulation of criminals and jihadists will continue to undermine Libyan and broader regional security. Improvements will take time and require building institutional capacity within the Libyan state as well as investments in monitoring capabilities, such as intelligence, surveillance, and reconnaissance platforms. Establishing an effective, modern border-management system, with all its legal and administrative requirements, will be far more difficult given the sorry state of Libya's legal and administrative structures. International efforts in this area exist but need to be greatly expanded if they are to have any impact.

Help Libya Build Its Public Administration

The personalistic nature of the Qaddafi regime left Libya with a severe lack of public administrative and bureaucratic structures. International actors are well positioned to help Libya improve its public administration, especially if the security situation improves. The EU and its member states are in a particularly good position for this task, due to their proximity to Libya. They should significantly increase their level of effort as soon as the security situation improves. As a temporary alternative, training in Europe should be encouraged. This training should include local as well as national-level institutions.

Acknowledgments

The authors owe great thanks to Karim and Khaled Mezran, Fred Wehrey, Jason Pack, Peter Cole, Anas El Gomati, and Wolfram Lacher for their stimulating discussions and advice on postwar developments in Libya. Thanks are also due to Keith Crane and Peter Mandaville, with whom we coauthored an earlier report that informed this monograph. Steve Watts and Alison Pargeter provided very thorough and particularly useful reviews.

We are also indebted to the several participants in an October 2012 RAND workshop, including from the UK Foreign Office, European Union, United Nations, Defense Department, State Department, White House, World Bank, International Monetary Fund, IHS, International Foundation for Electoral Systems, Dartmouth College, the National Endowment for Democracy, the International Republican Institute, National Democratic Institute, and the International Crisis Group.

We are grateful for the attention given to us during our field research in Libya by the European Union, United Nations, and U.S. Embassy and especially grateful to the members of the Libyan General National Congress who gave their time to meet with us in Tripoli. Thanks also to Mustafa Abushagur for his kind assistance in our research and to Ambassador Ali Aujali and his staff at the Libyan Embassy in Washington, D.C.

Christina Bartol played an important role in helping us research the chapter on economics and finalize the manuscript. Melissa Ko provided excellent support in the early stages of the project. George Willcoxon and David Stebbins both conducted valuable research on conflict trends presented herein. This work was funded through a generous grant from the Smith Richardson Foundation and we are also grateful to Nadia Shadlow for her considerable flexibility while we worked to get this project up and running.

Abbreviations

AQIM	al Qaeda in the Islamic Maghreb
EU	European Union
GDP	gross domestic product
GNC	General National Congress
JCP	Justice and Cooperation Party
LIFG	Libyan Islamic Fighting Group
LSF	Libyan Shield Forces
MANPADS	man-portable air defense systems
NATO	North Atlantic Treaty Organization
NFA	National Forces Alliance
NOC	National Oil Corporation
NTC	National Transitional Council
SSC	Supreme Security Committee
UN	United Nations
UNSMIL	United Nations Support Mission in Libya
WAC	Warriors Affairs Commission

CHAPTER ONE

Introduction

In late February 2011, Libya's population revolted against Muammar Qaddafi's four decades of dictatorship. Qaddafi threatened a brutal repression in response. After initial hesitations, NATO allies, acting under a mandate from the United Nations (UN) Security Council, attacked the regime and began a seven-month, low-intensity air campaign that eventually resulted in the demise of the regime. In August, Tripoli fell, and in October, Qaddafi was captured and killed by rebel forces.

After its war, Libya had a good deal going for it compared with other postconflict countries. The rebels had been largely unified, democratic political transitions in neighboring Tunisia and Egypt looked conducive to Libya's transition to peace, and Qaddafi had been utterly defeated. There seemed to be little risk that a pro-regime insurgency would develop, as it had, for example, in Iraq in the wake of Saddam Hussein's defeat.

The fact that Libya is a quarter of the size of Iraq in population and many times wealthier than Afghanistan also played to its favor. It had oil to sell and was close to Europe, which together should have helped ensure it did not drop completely off the radar in western capitals. Damage to its economic infrastructure was relatively light and even if regional, tribal, and other tensions existed, Libya's civil war differed from those in Bosnia, Kosovo, Syria, and other cases where ethnic or sectarian fighting had pitted citizens against each other in a fury of violence. This should have made postwar reconciliation easier. There was in fact fairly little violence immediately after the fall of Tripoli, and most indicators pointed to high levels of public support for the transition to peace.

In part because Libya's outlook seemed so positive after the war, the international strategy for post-conflict stabilization differed from that taken in all of NATO's prior military interventions in one important way: No peacekeeping or stabilization forces were deployed after the war. In general, the international footprint in Libya would be very limited, by historical standards. A small UN mission was given responsibility for coordinating international post-conflict stabilization support. Although many countries, including the United States, sent diplomats to help with the transition from war to peace, Libyans were largely left to fend for themselves.

The situation since then has been tumultuous and violent. Although there were some positive developments, including successful elections in July 2012, these were overshadowed by mounting violence that stunted efforts to establish functioning political institutions through which the Libyan people could realize their aspirations for self-rule. Jihadist groups—some linked to al Qaeda in the Islamic Maghreb (AQIM), an al Qaeda affiliate—meanwhile made use of the security vacuum to establish a foothold nationwide.

Libya today is thus in a very precarious situation, as are conditions in the broader Sahel and Maghreb regions. Jihadist activities in Mali, Tunisia, Algeria, and Egypt do not favor a rapid improvement in the outlook—although they are also not a reason to abandon Libya altogether. Indeed, these threats are one of the reasons the international community needs to take a more proactive approach to Libya's own evolution.

On one level, post-conflict Libya looks more and more like a cautionary tale of the inherent challenges postwar societies face. But given the very limited international contribution to post-conflict reconstruction, it should not be misrepresented as evidence of the futility of postwar reconstruction efforts themselves, much less of the initial military intervention or military intervention altogether. Political climate in the United States and many allied countries is unfortunately primed, after the challenges faced in Iraq and Afghanistan, to misinterpret the

Libya experience in precisely this way—with potentially adverse consequences for policy in Libya and future cases, such as Syria.

This study provides an overview of the main challenges Libya faced in the two years after its liberation, assesses the international effort, and identifies steps that could be taken now to improve Libya's future prospects. The remainder of this chapter explains the international strategy toward post-conflict reconstruction in Libya, and why it was so limited.

Chapters Two through Four focus on three major areas: security, statebuilding, and economic recovery, respectively. In each case, we examine the challenges that arose in the aftermath of the war, the measures taken to address them, the outcomes, and the consequences and implications for the overall stability effort.

Chapter Five looks at the situation today and assesses whether a different strategy, in particular involving the deployment of an interim international security force, might have had a positive impact.

Chapter Six identifies some initiatives that could improve Libya's future prospects.

The Post-Conflict Approach

Prior to Libya, NATO military interventions had normally been followed by post-conflict operations of significant size. In 1995, NATO deployed forces in Bosnia to safeguard the Dayton Accords. Soon thereafter, international actors set up an Office of the High Representative with executive authority to intervene in Bosnian politics to help implement the Accords' civilian aspects. In Kosovo in 1999, NATO followed up its air campaign with the deployment of peacekeeping forces and the UN set up a large civilian administrative structure to help manage postwar Kosovo's many challenges.

In the past two decades, the UN has also deployed peacekeeping forces and significant civilian post-conflict missions around the world. At the time the war in Libya ended, there were no fewer than 14 UN peacekeeping operations underway worldwide, varying in size from under 1,000 personnel in Cyprus to over 20,000 in the Democratic Republic of Congo.

For several reasons, however, the international role in Libya was limited and the majority of post-conflict reconstruction was left up to the Libyans themselves. First, because NATO adopted an airpower-heavy strategy, ground forces were limited to small numbers of special forces from Europe and the Gulf States. Precision airpower allowed NATO to avoid large numbers of civilian deaths, keep costs down, and ensure it was the rebels themselves who took the capital. The limited number of ground forces, however, also greatly reduced the extent of control and influence that NATO and its partners could exert after Qaddafi was gone. The question was whether to deploy forces, not whether to withdraw them.

Second, in contrast with NATO operations in Afghanistan and U.S. coalition operations in Iraq, the impetus for the intervention in Libya came in large part from France and Britain. Although President Obama supported the operation, he emphasized to his French and British counterparts that they would be expected to take the lead and bear as much of the cost as they could. The United States would support the effort, but provide only those capabilities it "uniquely" possessed. This arrangement also set the stage for a much-reduced U.S. role after the war.[1]

Third, within NATO, the operation was controversial. Allied participation was very low and seemed to be declining, despite the political approval from the North Atlantic Council, NATO's highest political body. Only half the alliance made military contributions and less than a third of the allies contributed to strike operations. Germany, one of the allies best placed to contribute to the intervention and post-conflict stabilization and reconstruction, voiced strong objections, abstained from the UN Security Council vote in protest, and ultimately opted out of military operations, even though it did not try to stop them

---

[1] Christopher S. Chivvis, *Toppling Qaddafi: Libya and the Limits of Liberal Intervention*, New York: Cambridge University Press, 2014, pp. 53–55.

(and eventually offered some diplomatic and financial support).[2] This controversy reduced the chances of a post-conflict role for the alliance.

Fourth, at the UN, fissures emerged on the Security Council over NATO's interpretation of the UN mandate soon after military operations began. Russia, China, and South Africa argued that NATO was exceeding the mandate approved in Resolution 1973 and had crossed the line between civilian protection and regime change. The resolution only provided for limited strikes to prevent violence against innocent civilians, they argued, but NATO was now actively seeking to overthrow Qaddafi. Although it was difficult to believe that these countries were as shocked as they claimed by NATO operations, the discord made further UN action on Libya—and for that matter Syria—difficult.[3]

Fifth, after the Iraq and Afghanistan wars, appetite for post-conflict deployments was very low in most western capitals. Europe was in the midst of a financial crisis and the United States was just emerging from one. Electoral cycles likely also played a role, and the Obama administration was no doubt wary of the risk that a quagmire in Libya could turn one of its main foreign policy victories into a target for reproach from Republicans, especially of the Tea Party, during a presidential election year.

Sixth, when it came to the specific question of a foreign troop presence, the Libyan interim authorities objected. During the war, the rebel leadership was largely opposed to foreign ground force deployments, calling only for air support and weapons. This pattern continued after the war. Many postwar rebel leaders were deeply concerned with their legitimacy, which they feared a foreign troop deployment would undermine. The last thing they wanted was to be seen as NATO's patsies. To complicate matters, Resolution 1973 specifically ruled out an "occupying force." When leaders on Libya's National Transitional Council (NTC) objected to post-conflict peacekeepers, discussion in NATO capitals fizzled.[4]

---

[2] Chivvis, 2014, pp. 59–64.

[3] Chivvis, 2014, pp. 175–179.

[4] Interviews with White House Staff, February 12, 2012; interview with former U.S. official, November 22, 2013.

These factors, combined with unexpected calm in Tripoli immediately after the war,[5] resulted in a very limited overall international approach to post-conflict reconstruction in Libya. On September 16, 2011, Security Council Resolution 2009 mandated the UN Support Mission in Libya (UNSMIL), under the leadership of UN Special Representative Ian Martin. The mandate called the mission to "assist and support" Libyan efforts to establish security, undertake political dialogue, extend state authority, promote and protect human rights, take steps to restart the economy, and coordinate the international effort. UNSMIL thus had no mandate to engage directly in Libyan politics, and with 200 total staff—many of which supporting the mission itself—it was limited in what it could accomplish.

In keeping with its wartime policy of focusing only on those areas where it had special capabilities, the United States took on special roles in certain areas, such as tracking and securing Qaddafi's weapons of mass destruction or man-portable air defense systems (MANPADS), which were believed to number several thousand. Like the UN, the European Union (EU) established a political mission only, rather than the far more robust civilian-military missions that it had deployed, for example, in Kosovo and elsewhere under its common security and defense policy. France, Britain, Italy, and other countries also established missions. Some of these deployed staff to help organize the now-chaotic Libyan ministries.

The essential tasks of establishing security, building political institutions, and restarting the economy, however, were left almost entirely up to Libya's new leaders themselves, who were also expected to foot most of the bill for reconstruction, not surprisingly given the country's oil wealth.

---

[5]   Interviews with White House Staff, February 17, 2012.

CHAPTER TWO

Security After the War

The need to establish a safe and secure environment after the war was widely recognized both by international actors and by the Libyan rebels' own postwar planning documents. A report undertaken under the auspices of the international contact group for Libya during the war, for example, noted the paramount importance of ensuring that "anti-Qaddafi militia do not evolve into armed wings of political factions, but are either merged into new, democratically accountable national security organizations or disarmed and demobilized."[1] Similarly, the UN's own initial study of the post-conflict planning environment noted the imperative that Libya "avoid chaos and ensure a sufficiently enabling environment for the fragile transition process to take hold."[2] UN Special Representative Ian Martin testified to the Security Council in December 2011 that "Unless the security situation is addressed quickly and effectively, interests of various stakeholders may become entrenched, undermining the legitimate authority of the State."[3] Sadly, foreknowledge of the challenge did not translate into effective action and security gradually deteriorated.

Achieving a secure environment had three basic parts. First, the armaments from the regime and the war needed to be cleaned up and

[1] International Stabilisation Response Team, Department for International Development (UK), "Libya: 20 May–30 June 2011," 2011.

[2] United Nations, *Consolidated Report of the Integrated Pre-Assessment Process for Libya Post-Conflict Planning*, Working Draft August 5, 2011, p.6.

[3] United Nations Security Council, "6698th Meeting Transcript," New York, UN Document S/PV/6698, December 22, 2011.

Libya's borders had to be secured. Second, Libya's national security sector needed to be reformed and rebuilt so that the armed services would be effective and support the transition to representative government. Third, the rebel militias that had won the war needed to be disarmed, demobilized, and reintegrated, either into civilian society or into Libya's new armed services.

Porous Borders and Widespread Arms

The country was awash in small arms and light weapons, including MANPADS, anti-tank missiles, Grad rockets, and mortars. France, Qatar, and other countries had also supplied the rebels with weapons during the war, with Qatar contributing more than 20,000 tons of weapons, including assault rifles, rocket-propelled grenades, and other small arms.[4] Qatar and France both also supplied the rebels with Milan anti-tank missiles.[5] More important were Qaddafi's own weapon stocks, most of which had been let loose during the war. The UN estimated that, at the time of Qaddafi's overthrow, Libya's armed forces held between 250,000 and 700,000 firearms, the majority of which (70–80 percent) were assault rifles.[6] MI6 estimated that there were a million tons of weaponry in Libya, more than the entire arsenal of the British army.[7] These weapons now threatened Libya's security.

Large numbers of MANPADS and the remnants of Qaddafi's nuclear weapons program, meanwhile, posed a threat beyond Libya. Qaddafi had purchased as many as 20,000 Soviet MANPADS, a stunning number that would be a major challenge to track down and

---

[4]   Sam Dagher, Charles Levinson, and Margaret Coker, "Tiny Kingdom's Huge Role in Libya Draws Concern," *Wall Street Journal*, October 17, 2011.

[5]   Ian Black, Chris McGreal, and Harriet Sherwood, "Libyan Rebels Supplied with Anti-Tank Weapons by Qatar" *The Guardian*, April 14, 2011; Richard Spencer, "France Supplying Weapons to Libyan Rebels" *The Telegraph*, June 29, 2011.

[6]   United Nations, "Transnational Organized Crime in West Africa," undated.

[7]   Mark Hookham, "MI6 Warns Libyan Arms Dumps Are 'Tesco for World Terrorists,'" *The Sunday Times*, June 16, 2013.

collect. The United States funded the program to recover the MAN-PADS, although it was reportedly run by South African contractors.[8] Meanwhile, there were 6,400 known barrels of partially processed uranium (yellowcake) stored in Libya in a facility near Sabha in the south, loosely guarded by a Libyan army battalion.[9] Libya also had not completed the process of destroying its chemical weapons stocks, and only 51 percent of its original mustard gas stockpile of 24.7 metric tons had been destroyed by the time the regime was overthrown.[10] (Although this task was successful completed in early 2014).

Because Libya's borders were so long and porous, these loose weapons were a threat to the broader region and beyond. Getting control of Libya's 1,680-mile southern border was an enormous task, however.[11] Qaddafi had sought to control—or perhaps influence—the border largely by establishing alliances with tribes that regularly moved back and forth across it. Building a modern border system required not only technological capabilities, such as unmanned aerial vehicles and other monitoring systems, but also staffing, effective administrative structures, and good inter-governmental coordination. Libya might hope to use its oil wealth to acquire the necessary technologies, but the manpower and administrative needs for effective border control were a bigger challenge given the disarray of Libya's state institutions.

The Need for Far-Reaching Security Sector Reform

The Libyan state was in no position to provide security for its population after the war. Before it could do so, it needed far-reaching security

---

[8] "Thousands of Libyan Missiles from Qaddafi Era Missing in Action," *CBS News*, March 25, 2013.

[9] "UN Envoy Says 6,400 Barrels of Yellowcake Is Stored in Libya" *BBC News*, December 10, 2013; Anthony Loyd, "Al-Qa'ida Eyes Gaddafi's Missiles and Uranium," *The Australian*, October 23, 2013.

[10] Organization for the Prohibition of Chemical Weapons, "Libya: Facts and Figures," undated.

[11] Charles Bremner and Wil Crisp, "Chaos Turns Libya into Back Door for Migrants," *The Times*, October 17, 2013, p. 37.

sector reform coupled with disarmament, demobilization, and reintegration of rebel forces. This has proven impossible.

Ideally, security sector reform takes place according to a top-down blueprint that lays out priorities and determines how the institutions that govern the security sector at the highest levels will be organized. Libya's postwar leaders had had no time to consider such questions, however, and in most cases lacked any background necessary for thinking through issues such as how to ensure civilian control of the armed forces and whether to establish a national security council for decisionmaking.

Indeed, in the prevailing conditions after Qaddafi's fall, the salience of such issues was fairly distant. Civilian control of the military was surely desired by most, if not all, Libyans, but how exactly that would work or even what it meant was still to be determined. Building a national security framework to support peaceful transition was especially difficult, given the absence of any certainty about what Libya's governing political institutions would look like. As a result, rational, top-down security sector reform was nearly impossible.

Moreover, the institutions of the security sector were extremely weak or non-existent administratively. The Ministry of Interior was weak to start with and would weaken further after the war. Worse, the Ministry of Defense had actually been dis-established by Qaddafi decades ago. The military had been run by the Chief of Staff, creating an inherent tension in efforts to build a more standard Ministry of Defense.

The prewar military staff was also extremely weak. Ever wary of possible coup threats, Qaddafi constantly shook up the ranks, moved officers around arbitrarily, and doled out posts by patronage requirements rather than merit. Promotions from the lower ranks were pro-forma and very few new officers were added after the 1993 coup attempt. As a result, the upper ranks were badly bloated.[12] Only a few were allowed to rise above Qaddafi's own rank of colonel. There was

---

[12] Interview with U.S. official, Washington, D.C., October 2, 2012. See also, Dirk Vandewalle, *History of Modern Libya*, New York: Cambridge University Press, 2012, pp.119–150.

no capacity for decisionmaking, strategic analysis, or planning, all of which are needed for successful security sector reform.

Defeated in battle and neglected under Qaddafi, what remained of the military forces themselves were also very weak. Prewar Libyan security services were estimated to number some 76,000, but in reality totaled only 20,000.[13] The Qaddafi military had been designed for armored warfare in the desert and included large numbers of Soviet tanks, artillery, and armored vehicles. In addition to being of questionable need for the threats now facing Libya, most of this equipment was in poor condition. The navy was barely operational and had been damaged by NATO during the war. The air force had a variety of fixed-wing aircraft, but it lacked training. Training for the regime's helicopter squadron was only somewhat better. The most sophisticated weapon systems had gone to Qaddafi's 32nd Brigade, headed by Qaddafi's son Khamis. This brigade had been responsible for most of the regime fighting during the war and had therefore been the most heavily targeted by NATO. Training and development programs that could strengthen the force, especially at the lower levels, were non-existent, as were systems for budgeting and other critical procedures.

The state of Libya's legal and penitential system was almost as bad, and a major backlog of court cases soon developed. There were over 5,000 people in various forms of custody nationwide, according to Human Rights Watch. The police were functioning minimally, but in many areas officers were afraid to go out in uniform. Others simply did not show up for work at all, especially in eastern towns such as Benghazi and Derna, where recriminatory assassinations of police soon were soon to become common.[14]

A Misratan leader, Fawzi Abdel Al, took control of the Ministry of Interior, while a powerful Zintani militia leader, Osama al-Juwaili, became minister of defense. The Chief of Defense position went to Yousef al-Mangoush, a high-ranking regime defector.[15] These individu-

---

[13] Florence Gaub, "Libya: The Struggle for Security," *EUISS Brief,* June 2013.

[14] Interview with Libyan government official, Tripoli, February 6, 2013.

[15] Robert M. Perito and Alison Laporte-Oshiro, "Libya: Security Sector Reconstruction," *United States Institute of Peace,* July 5, 2012.

als and their successors enjoyed varying degrees of support for their efforts, but political support for security sector reform in general was weak, given the stakes involved and growing uncertainty about Libya's future. Without a constitution or a clear vision of what Libya's future would look like and who would be in power, willingness to make bold decisions about the security services was almost non-existent. Meanwhile, the committees within the postwar government charged with responsibility for security-related issues operated in an uncoordinated manner and were often at odds with each other, further slowing reform efforts.[16]

The UN has done what it could to help the security situation, but with very limited results. It helped the Ministry of Defense develop a white paper on security sector reform, but while the paper likely helped to build some limited awareness of the challenges the country faced, the implementation of any of the recommendations contained therein—for example, regarding doctrine, organization, training, etc.—face immense obstacles.

As one international official put it, UNSMIL was "mandated to provide advice and assist the Libyan government in developing professional and sustainable security institutions under civilian oversight and in accordance with democratic principles. UNSMIL did this quite well in terms of the provision of advice, but without either viable state security forces or an international stabilization force to maintain security, the implementation of security sector reform initiatives proved ineffective."[17]

Some European countries undertook to build capacity within the security ministries through partnering arrangements, but these efforts were small scale and would only yield results over the long term. There was a program to train Libyan police in Jordan, but it got off to a rough start when rioting and infighting between the recruits broke out and many had to be sent back to Libya.[18]

---

[16] Interview with Libyan government official, Tripoli, February 6, 2013.

[17] Interview with international official, Washington, D.C., November, 2013.

[18] Abdul-Jalil Mustafa, "Libyan Police Trainees Arrested in Jordan After Riots and Arson," *Libya Herald*, July 11, 2012.

Libya thus needed—and still needs—a far-reaching overhaul of its security institutions if it were to become a functioning modern state. Providing security to the Libyan people and preventing violence between armed groups fell to the revolutionaries' brigades that had fought in the war and other groups that sprung up in its aftermath—these groups, however, were also a major source of insecurity.

Armed Groups After the War

The rebel forces that overthrew Qaddafi were highly fragmented and the idea of a unified "rebel army" was purely fictional. The official rebel army was composed largely of former regime military members that defected to the rebel side in the early days of the uprising, and its membership was limited mostly to Benghazi and other eastern areas the regime vacated early in the war. It was stuck in the east for most of the war anyway, unable to break through the front at the town of Brega, which lies to the southwest of Benghazi along the main coastal road toward Tripoli and Libya's other major cities.

The military advances that actually brought the regime down were the product of organic uprisings elsewhere in the country, especially in Misrata and in the Nafusah mountains, which lie in the west along the border with Tunisia. When the war ended, the brigades from these various areas occupied territory around the country. They were not at odds with one another, but they were also far from united.

Estimates of the total number of armed groups in Libya after the war have varied significantly, in part because of differences of definition. Most estimates run in the low hundreds,[19] although some assessments found several hundred in single cities alone, such as Misrata.[20] What constituted an armed group has been an issue for debate and

---

[19] For example, Karim Mezran and Fadel Lamen, "Security Challenges to Libya's Quest for Democracy," *Atlantic Council Issue Brief,* September 2012; International Crisis Group, "Holding Libya Together: Security Challenges After Qadhafi," Crisis Group Middle East/North Africa Report No. 115, December 14, 2011.

[20] Brian McQuinn, *After the Fall: Libya's Evolving Armed Groups,* Geneva, Switzerland: Small Arms Survey, October 2012b.

different terms have been used, including militia, brigade (*khatiba*), or simply armed group.

Whatever terminology one choses, however, it is clear that there are a number of different types of armed groups, with differing histories, capabilities, and intentions. At one end, there are the rebel brigades that fought during the war. These brigades are themselves differentiated by regional and tribal allegiances as well as by capabilities and geographic location. There were also groups that were not rebel fighting forces, in the sense that they had not engaged in fighting against the regime but were formed instead to address local security problems in the wake of the war. In addition to these, criminal gangs emerged either during the war or after, along with jihadist groups, especially in the east. Most estimates indicate that such groups are small, even if problematic and growing.[21]

In many regions or towns, the revolutionary groups coalesced under military councils during or shortly after the war. These councils took control of local security. The authority of the councils varied, however, with the main loyalties of the rank and file normally remaining with the commanders with whom they had fought. After the war, the councils often acted as militaries in being, issuing identification cards, establishing internal procedures for keeping the peace, securing their arsenals, and reinforcing their command and control structures.[22]

Many of these groups were fairly well armed. Although there had been serious shortages of weapons early in the war, as the war progressed, rebels obtained weapons from external sponsors and by capturing regime casernes. By the end of the war, these weapons included small arms, such as AK-47s; machine guns; and rocket-propelled grenades. They also included smaller (14.5 mm) and medium-sized (20–33 mm) anti-aircraft machine guns that were affixed to the back of pickup trucks, and some pieces of artillery. The most substantial equipment the rebels controlled were tanks, largely Soviet-era T-55s, although their ability to use these more-sophisticated systems was limited, given a lack of training. Many of these weapons were acquired in the final

---

[21] For example, see McQuinn, 2012b.

[22] International Crisis Group, 2011.

weeks of the war, after Tripoli fell, when rebels who descended on the capital looted the regime's warehouses and then took the weapons back to their home bases.[23]

While it is clear in retrospect that a few of these armed groups—especially the jihadists in the east—were already a direct threat to security at the end of the war, the majority of the revolutionary brigade leaders were not. They espoused their good intentions and desire to protect the revolution. In most cases they also expressed their willingness to disarm. Many cited concerns about their own security or lack of trust in other groups or the NTC's ability to shepherd Libya toward a free future as the main reasons they had not yet put down their arms. A commander in the western mountains, for example, argued that he would not disarm until the country had "a civil constitution and democratic system."[24] One commander from Misrata similarly argued that he was "not after any political, economic, or financial benefits" and supported the legitimacy of the NTC, but was unwilling to disarm before the country was "run by those who deserve to run it."[25]

Some militia leaders simply pointed out that if they disarmed and disbanded, there would be no one at all in control of security in their areas and the population would be put at risk of predation from criminal groups and other malfeasants. In general, tensions between these groups were not particularly serious, even if levels of trust were low. Popular support for peace among the population was meanwhile very

---

[23] See, for example, Peter Osborne, "With Gaddafi Gone, Who Will Run the New Libya?" *The Telegraph*, October 20, 2011; Peter Goodspeed, "Libyan Weapons May Soon Be in Terrorist Hands," *National Post*, September 9, 2011, p. A1; Slobodan Lekic, "NATO Urges Libyan Authorities to Seize Arms Caches," Associated Press, October 3, 2011; McQuinn, 2012b; International Crisis Group, 2011.

[24] David D. Kirkpatrick, "In Turnaround, Libyan Militias Want to Keep Their Arms," *International Herald Tribune*, November 3, 2011, p. 5.

[25] See, for example, Amanda Kadlec, "A Stable Transition in Tripoli, Actually," *The Daily Star*, February 21, 2012. This was a fairly widely held view voiced in public and private by many international officials in author interviews conducted in NATO capitals in late 2011 and early 2012.

strong, limiting the range for aggressive action by any one particular militia.[26]

Skirmishes did take place, especially in Tripoli, which was occupied by multiple brigades, many of which distrusted each other. The Misratans controlled the port, the Zintanis controlled the airport, and Berber groups from the west controlled Martyrs' Square. The interim prime minister's convoy was attacked in November, for example, and fighting also broke out between Zintani brigades and the national army over the Zintani's occupation of the airport.[27] On the whole, however, calm prevailed in the early months after the end of the war, notwithstanding great uncertainty about the future.

The Breakdown of the Rebel Disarmament Effort

Disarming and consolidating control of these armed groups was a priority for Abdul Raheem Al-Keeb's interim government from the moment it took the oath of office on November 24, but the challenges involved in doing so proved insurmountable. Although disarming the rebel groups was widely recognized as a priority from the international perspective as well as that of the Libyan authorities, UNSMIL was limited in the role that it could play, both by its mandate, which did not give it executive authority to intervene in Libyan politics and decision-making, and by its limited staff.

One problem was that NTC had no reliable military forces—Libyan or international—backing it and therefore had to rely almost entirely on financial and other incentives to persuade the armed groups to either disarm or join the ranks of the army and police. A strategy of forcibly coercing the rebel brigades to join the military obviously would not have been advisable, but government overtures to rebel leaders to disarm or cooperate more actively in protecting the political pro-

---

[26] Simon Denyer, "Libyan Militias Amass Weapons from Unsecured Depots," *Washington Post*, September 22, 2011, p. A11.

[27] International Crisis Group, 2011.

cess would have carried more weight had they been backed by the possibility of coercion either by government or outside forces.

Immediately after the war, an inter-ministerial Warriors Affairs Commission (WAC) was established for rebel demobilization and reintegration. It distributed registration forms nationwide through the military councils and major brigade leadership, and was soon overwhelmed with registrations from youths eager to take advantage of the generous payments and other compensations offered. By the end of February 2012, it had received 148,000 registrations.[28] Bureaucratic capacity to handle such a surfeit of demand was extremely low.[29] Moreover, the wave of youths registering suggested that a significant portion were not in fact veterans, but simply unemployed youths seeking jobs.

In reality, the distinction between a "real" and a "phony" rebel could be difficult to make, given the variety of roles that many rebels played in the war. This would further complicate the process. Only 6,000 of those who registered with the WAC wanted to be integrated into the regular armed forces; 2,200 wanted to join the border police, and 11,000 the oil guards. In contrast, 44,000 wanted civil-service jobs and 78,000 wanted to start their own businesses. Over two-thirds did not have college educations, however, which made their demands even more difficult to meet.[30] Although the WAC later complained of not getting the funding it needed from Tripoli, this was in part due to suspicions about its favoritism for some groups over others.

As the WAC struggled to handle the crush of job applications, the Ministry of Interior and the Ministry of Defense initiated separate registration programs, complicating the overall national process. Both ministries were populated in part by revolutionaries and in part by former functionaries. Naturally, the top leadership of the ministries was largely in the hands of revolutionaries, but these new leaders often had little or no administrative experience or understanding of the daunting challenges of security sector reform. Furthermore, they

---

[28] United Nations Security Council, "Ian Martin's Report at the 6728th Session of the UN Security Council on February 29, 2012," UN Document S/PV.6728, February 29, 2012.

[29] Al Jaazeera interview with Al-Shuwayli, January 2012.

[30] Gaub, 2013.

were preoccupied primarily with securing power and benefits for their own regions. The security ministries as a whole meanwhile remained suspect in the eyes of the brigades, on account of their former roles as part of Qaddafi's apparatus of repression.

The Ministry of Interior's approach was to establish a body called the Supreme Security Committee (SSC), which brought together several revolutionary groups. In theory, the creation of the SSC would allow skeptical revolutionaries to supplement or supplant the existing police, within the outlines of a new Libyan state. The SSC set up offices around the country and paid a good stipend to those who agreed to join. This brought some 100,000 revolutionaries under its purview within the next few months.[31] Because these rebels were integrated as complete units, however, and because the state was inherently weak and unable to discipline them, they continued to operate largely as independent forces, just as they had before.

Moreover, some of the brigades that were incorporated into the SSC, such as the radical Islamist Abu Salim Martyrs Brigade from the eastern town of Derna, which came under the SSC umbrella in June 2012, were inherently problematic. While the purported absorption of such groups into the state gave an appearance of progress and growing order, the underlying reality remained that it was one of many militias operating independently and according to its own interests and objectives. If anything, bringing such groups into the SSC tent reinforced their legitimacy and authority, without furthering the goal of unifying the national forces. The SSC became increasingly viewed as aligned with Islamist political forces and, in some cases, even with jihadists. Members of the SSC were involved in the unlawful destruction of Sufi shrines in 2012 (Figure 2.1), the attacks on government ministries in 2013, and other acts of violence. Although militias under the SSC can now be seen providing nominal police functions in Tripoli and elsewhere, they have too often been a threat to security. Their continued autonomy creates uncertainty and instability.

---

[31] Frederic Wehrey, "Libya's Militia Menace: The Challenge After the Elections," *Foreign Affairs*, July 12, 2012a.

Figure 2.1
Razed Sufi Shrine, Tripoli

SOURCE: Photo by Christopher Chivvis.
RAND RR577-2.1

The Ministry of Defense also attempted a program of national registration, offering one-time payments to rebels who participated. Registration came with no immediate requirements, however, and many groups decided to register more than once.[32] The registration program was suspended in April 2012, at which point the Ministry of Defense recognized an existing rebel umbrella organization that went by the name Libyan Shield Forces (LSF). As with the SSC, however, recognizing the LSF did not necessarily ensure the loyalty of its forces to the Defense Minister, Shuwayli, or the Army Chief of Staff, General Mangoush.

---

[32] International Crisis Group, "Divided We Stand," Middle East/North Africa Report No. 130, September 14, 2012.

What emerged instead was an ad hoc arrangement in which LSF would provide forces at the behest of the government on a provisional basis and with varying degrees of effectiveness. LSF forces proved willing to rent themselves out to the government to address the conflicts in the south, but have also stormed government buildings and are rumored to have been involved in criminal activities, such as smuggling. Like the SSC, their autonomy is an inherent source of insecurity and potential violence.

These efforts failed either to significantly reduce the availability of weapons or unify the rebel forces under state authority. Libyan government officials have promised on several occasions since to disarm or dismantle the militias, but to no avail. In the aftermath of the Benghazi attacks, for example, President of the General National Congress (GNC) Mohamed al-Magariaf said militias would have to 48 hours to disarm or face consequences.[33] A few months later, as militias intensified their pressure on the political discussion in Tripoli, the Interior Ministry announced "Operation Tripoli" to clear the capital of armed gangs.[34] Then, in June, after a spate of violence in Benghazi, Libya's Army Chief of Staff, Col. Salem al-Gnaidy, said militias would have to lay down their arms or join the army by the end of the year.[35] None of these efforts has had any significant effect.

The Proliferation of Conflicts

With no central authority, a heavily armed populace, and a stalled disarmament, demobilization and reintegration process, conflict began to proliferate nationwide (Figure 2.2) a few months after the end of the war. Violence took multiple forms, ranging from tribal disputes over

---

[33] Mel Frykberg, "Libya's Vow to Reign in Militias Is Immediately Challenged," *Christian Science Monitor*, September 24, 2012.

[34] "Ministries of Interior and Defence Move to Stamp Out Renegade Militias," *Libya Herald*, March 19, 2013.

[35] Essam Mohamed and Jamel Arfaoui, "Libya: Ultimatum Issued to Militias," *Maghrebia*, June 13, 2013.

Figure 2.2
Conflict Incidents and Fatalities in Libya, November 2011 to October 2013

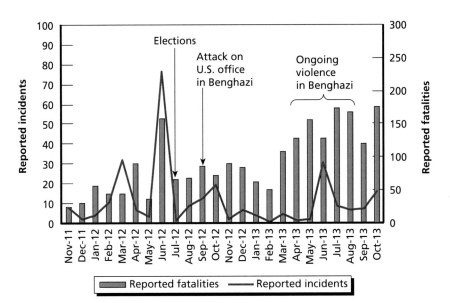

SOURCE: Armed Conflict Location Event Database. See Clionadh Raleigh, Andrew Linke, Håvard Hegre, and Joakim Karlsen, "Introducing ACLED-Armed Conflict Location and Event Data," *Journal of Peace Research*, Vol. 47, No. 5, 2010, pp. 1–10.
RAND RR577-2.2

territory and trading routes, to conflicts with alleged regime holdouts, to score settling, federalist maneuvering, and jihadist efforts to generally destabilize the country.

Much of the violence in the first half of 2012 revolved either around fighting between the revolutionaries and alleged holdouts of the Qaddafi regime or between the tribes on Libya's periphery. The loci of violence were the towns of Sirte, Tarhouna, and especially Bani Walid.

Located to the southeast of Tripoli, these towns had been Qaddafi's last holdouts after the fall of the capital. After Qaddafi's death they surrendered, and pro-revolutionary brigades and military councils were installed. These councils comported themselves largely as occupiers, however, and from November 2011 through January 2012, tensions between them and town citizens escalated. According to Bani

Walid residents, the May 28 Brigade, the pro-revolutionary force in control of that town, regularly harassed and otherwise mistreated the townspeople. Residents also cited the NTC's deficient efforts to repair the damage done to the town during the siege and failure to restore basic services.[36]

On January 23, 2012, the tension erupted into violent clashes and the May 23 Brigade was chased out of Bani Walid. Some residents raised Qaddafi's flag, sparking alarm that the war was restarting. The Deputy UN Special Representative and the Defense Minister Juwayli were both dispatched to calm the situation. Meanwhile, rebels began to converge on the site, raring for a fight and eager to punish the upstart town. Holding back the rebel forces on the one hand, and facing recrimination in Tripoli on the other, Juwayli and others managed to negotiate an agreement that would leave a non-revolutionary council in control.[37]

The immediate flare-up was over, but the underlying problem did not go away. In July, a Misratan rebel named Omran Shabaan, who was credited with having captured Qaddafi just prior to his demise, was kidnapped and held prisoner in Bani Walid for two months. Misrata's leaders charged that Bani Walid residents were torturing him, and he died in September while undergoing treatment for wounds in a hospital in Paris.

Enraged, Misratan brigades marched on Bani Walid and again besieged it, justifying their onslaught as a much-needed purge of the country's last pro-Qaddafi holdout. To a certain degree this was not untrue, but many observers pointed to longstanding differences between Misrata and the towns of this region as equally important in the score-settling. The government authorized the attack, but only

---

[36] Liam Stack, "Pro-Government Libyan Militia Routed from a Qaddafi Bastion," *The New York Times*, January 24, 2012.

[37] Taha Zargoun and Oliver Holmes, "Libyan Official in Talks with Unruly Town," *Washington Post*, January 26, 2012; Nick Meo and Hassan Morajea, "Militia Chaos in Bani Walid Raises Danger of Civil War in post-Gaddafi Libya," *The Telegraph*, January 28, 2012; "Bani Walid Fighters Stage Sit-in, Call for Libyan Defence Minister's Dismissal," *BBC Monitoring Middle East*, January 28, 2012.

because it was helpless to do otherwise. When the violence ended in late October, 22 people had died and hundreds more had been injured.[38]

Flare-ups of violence in western and especially southern Libya over the course of 2012 also left many dead, as fear and insecurity continued to reign and groups were left to themselves to vie for resources.

The most violent incidents occurred between Tebu and Arab tribes in Sebha on March 26, where heavy fighting left 147 people dead and approximately 500 wounded.[39] The Tebu are a nomadic black Sahara desert tribe that was often discriminated against under Qaddafi. Violence erupted between them and the Arab Awlad Sulayman and Awlad Seif tribes and reached new heights of barbarity when a peace council deteriorated into a firefight between the groups in Sebha's town hall.[40]

Recrimination and blame for the violence was mutual, but the deeper roots were a struggle for control over local resources and security. With Qaddafi gone, the Awlad Sulayman, who had supported the revolution, had been pushing to consolidate control over the town and thereby gain dominance in the broader southern region. The Tebu, for their part, feared further discrimination and potential expulsion from the smuggling routes on which their livelihood depended.[41]

The NTC quickly dispatched a contingent of 3,000 regular army and LSF forces from Benghazi, along with negotiators in an effort to contain the outbreak of violence.[42] A council of local elders spearheaded a reconciliation process between the feuding tribes. Calm prevailed within a few days, but underlying tensions persisted. In May, in an effort to assert its control, the NTC declared Sebha part of a southern "military zone"—although it was unclear what this actually meant

---

[38] Kareem Fahim, "Libyan Town Under Siege Is a Center of Resistance to the New Government," *The New York Times*, October 21, 2012a; Kareem Fahim, "Libyan Forces Now Control Restive Town, Officials Say," *The New York Times*, October 24, 2012b.

[39] United Nations, "Report of the Secretary General on the United Nations Support Mission in Libya," UN Document S/201/675, August 30, 2012.

[40] International Crisis Group, 2012.

[41] "Libya: Uneasy Calm in Sebha After Clashes" *IRIN*, May 14, 2012.

[42] "Libyan Official Says 50 Killed, 150 Injured in Sebha Clashes," *BBC Monitoring Middle East*, March 28, 2012.

in practice, given the government's inability to enforce the declaration on its own.

Lower-level violence there and elsewhere would continue. On April 21, fighting in Kufra left 44 dead and 150 wounded in similar clashes between Tebu and Arab tribes. Violence between other groups occurred in Zuwara in the west, in Ghadamis along the border with Tunisia, and in Zintan, leaving many others dead and wounded over the course of the year.[43]

These conflicts took a serious toll on Libya's political stabilization. For one, as discussed in Chapter Three, they distracted and further encumbered the work of the already overloaded transitional authorities in Tripoli. They also increased the power of militias aligned with the LSF, and especially the Benghazi LSF forces, who were called upon to put down the clash in Sebha. These forces gained prestige, experience, and compensation for their cooperation—all of which came at Tripoli's expense. Most of all, the violence underscored how feeble the national army really was and made the Tripoli authorities appear feckless and impotent, further eroding their authority and legitimacy.

Jihadism and al Qaeda in Libya

These conflicts simmered in the first year after the fall of Tripoli, but attracted nowhere near the global attention of the attack on U.S. diplomatic compounds in Benghazi on September 11, 2012, that killed U.S. Ambassador Chris Stevens along with three other Americans. The Benghazi attacks ignited a firestorm of finger-pointing in Washington and enormously complicated the already failing task of moving Libya toward self-sustaining peace and security.

In the aftermath of Benghazi, attention in Washington focused on who had said what and when rather than on assessing the underlying causes of Libya's security deterioration and what might be done to reverse it. Meanwhile, on the ground, the United States and its European allies were forced to severely restrict their movement and contact

---

[43] United Nations, 2012.

with the Libyan people, ensuring that the light international footprint would become no international footprint, especially in the roiling eastern province.

Even prior to the Benghazi attacks, signs of new threats to security in both Benghazi and Tripoli had become visible. Individual terrorist-style attacks targeted against symbols of authority were becoming more frequent. There were car bombings and guerilla-style attacks on government buildings in both cities, for example, and in Benghazi the British Ambassador narrowly escaped death when a rocket-propelled grenade fired at his car failed to detonate.[44]

Libyan officials claimed that Qaddafi supporters were behind these attacks, but most evidence pointed to the jihadists. Individual cases of jihadism might be found anywhere in Libya, but the social and historical conditions in the east are particularly conducive to militancy, and the east had been a center of jihadist activities for decades.

In the 1980s several individuals had travelled from there to fight against the Soviets in Afghanistan. Many banded together to form the Libyan Islamic Fighting Group (LIFG), which soon took up arms against the Qaddafi regime. Qaddafi crushed their uprising, however, capturing many LIFG adherents and incarcerating them in Tripoli's notorious Abu Salim prison. Many of those who escaped capture fled abroad, either back to Afghanistan or elsewhere. Some of these individuals fought alongside al Qaeda.

Abdel Hakim Belhaj was the most frequently cited exemplar of this milieu. A former member of LIFG, Belhaj was captured by MI6 in 2004 and claims to have been rendered and tortured before being sent back to Libya, where he was locked up in Abu Salim. He subsequently renounced violence and was released from prison, along with other members of LIFG, in 2010 under an amnesty program spearheaded by Qaddafi's son Saif.

When the revolution broke out, however, Belhaj was quick to join the rebels and soon found himself at the head of one of the largest rebel forces. He owed his military success in part to support from Qatar,

---

[44] See Christopher Chivvis, "A Year after the Fall of Tripoli, Libya Still Fragile," CNN.com, August 23, 2012.

which turned out to be a double-edged sword when he made a run for office in the July 2012 parliamentary elections and was soundly defeated—in part because he was viewed as being too closely linked to a foreign government.

Former jihadists like Belhaj played an important role during the revolution, if for no reason other than that they had fighting experience that most Libyans lacked. It is true that their importance to the rebel victory can be overstated and their role in the fighting may have been exaggerated both by Qaddafi and by some media outlets, such as *Al Jazeera*.[45] Nevertheless, in the east, there were many Islamists who saw the revolution as an opening to an Islamic state under *shari'a*, and were keen on ensuring progress in this direction when the revolt was over. Militants with varying degrees of commitment to jihad took advantage of the complete absence of government security forces to put down roots, settle old scores, and promote their cause. They have resisted efforts by the state to reassert control, and their very existence seriously complicates the problem of reconstruction and stabilization.

The numbers of jihadists in Libya are not large and should not be exaggerated. There is also little evidence that jihadists enjoy the support of even the more conservative Islamist political parties. To the contrary, pacifist conservatives, often from an older generation, coexist uneasily alongside the more radical crowd. The climate of religious conservatism in the east makes it somewhat easier for the militants to operate, but the landscape of militancy in eastern Libya is shifting and kaleidoscopic.

Ansar al Sharia in Benghazi is a prime example. Members of the group were reported in the *Wall Street Journal* to have telephoned AQIM after the Benghazi attack to brag about their exploits.[46] This was too easily interpreted in some media coverage as straightforward

---

[45] See Noman Benotman, Jason Pack, and James Brandon, "Islamists," in Jason Pack, ed., *The 2011 Libyan Uprisings and the Struggle for the Post-Qadhafi Future*, New York: Palgrave, 2013, pp. 191–228.

[46] Margaret Coker, "Militant Suspected in Attack in Libya Remains at Large," *Wall Street Journal*, October 17, 2012, p. A1.

evidence that al Qaeda was behind the attack and, by implication, running an operation in Libya.

The reality is more complicated. To begin with, the fact that Ansar Al Sharia called AQIM is no indication that AQIM was behind the attack—only that some members of the Libyan group looked to AQIM for encouragement and legitimacy. More importantly, the link between AQIM itself and the al Qaeda of Osama bin Laden is, to date, rather weak. Although AQIM draws inspiration from bin Laden's message and has clearly cooperated with the core of al Qaeda on occasion, its objectives have remained largely local and limited to the Maghreb and Sahel regions of North Africa. Whereas bin Laden's threat was primarily global, AQIM's is primarily local—although AQIM rhetoric has sometimes targeted European allies.[47]

This is by no means, however, to deny the growing relationship between militant Islam in Libya and al Qaeda's African franchises, much less to downplay Libya's militant problem, which remains very serious—especially when it comes to Libya's security outlook.

Abu Khattala, an avowed al Qaeda sympathizer, leader of a brigade known as the Abu Obeida Bin Jarrah Brigade, and key instigator of the Benghazi attack, is a case in point. Khattala continued to operate freely outside the reach of the Tripoli government after the attack, giving interviews to journalists on the veranda of Benghazi hotels. He insisted that while he was not formally a member of al Qaeda, he was a big supporter.[48]

There have also been public reports that even during the revolution al Qaeda operative Abdul Basit Azuz had been sent to Libya by al Qaeda chief Ayman Zawahiri to take advantage of the revolution and find new recruits. Azuz set up camp in Derna and began recruiting

---

[47] Christopher S. Chivvis and Andrew Liepman, *North Africa's Menace: AQIM's Evolution and the U.S. Policy Response,* Santa Monica, Calif.: RAND Corporation, RR-415-OSD, 2013.

[48] David D. Kirkpatrick, "Suspect in Libya Attack, in Plain Sight, Scoffs at U.S.," *The New York Times,* October 18, 2012b, p. A1; David D. Kirkpatrick, "A Deadly Mix in Benghazi," *New York Times,* December 28, 2013, p. A1.

and training fighters, possibly as far west as Brega.[49] Derna itself was a longstanding hotbed of radicalism, believed by the U.S. army to have sent more fighters to Iraq than any other single town in the world.[50]

As noted above, other individuals, such as Bin Qumu, closely linked to al Qaeda also operate from there. Training camps in Derna are now expected to be a major source of training for fighters headed to wage jihad in other countries, Syria above all. Conservative Muslim representatives from the town acknowledge its problems, but argue that they are simply the result of a lack of job opportunities for local youths. They also claim that the problem stems in part from the weakness of traditional tribal structures in what was once a comparatively cosmopolitan port city.[51] Whatever the cause, the activities of jihadists in Derna have become cause for concern, in Libya as well as in the United States and Europe.

In the aftermath of the Benghazi attack, the government in Tripoli insisted that it was determined to take action against the militias. Public outrage was at an all-time high, and some hoped that the silver lining in the tragedy would be a concerted effort to re-establish some modicum of state control in the region. Without loyal security forces, internally divided, and increasingly under pressure from armed gangs milling around outside the government buildings, the possibilities for assertive government action, however, were extremely limited. More than a year after the Benghazi attack, the situation has not improved. If anything, the inroads of the Islamist militants have increased.

To begin with, terrorist attacks, which in the first year after the war were largely confined to the east, spread to Tripoli in 2013. There were several small incidents of attacks on government buildings and officials, but the most dramatic was a car bomb that exploded outside the French Embassy, injuring two guards and destroying the build-

---

[49] Nic Robertson, Paul Cruickshank, and Tim Lister, "Growing Concern over Jihadist 'Safe Haven' in Eastern Libya," CNN.com, May 15, 2012.

[50] David D. Kirkpatrick, "Libya Democracy Clashes With Fervor for Jihad," *The New York Times*, June 23, 2012a, p.A1.

[51] Interview with Muslim Brotherhood parliamentary representative from Derna, Tripoli, Libya, February 5, 2013 (name withheld on request).

ing. That attack was widely viewed as retribution by AQIM-linked groups for France's January intervention to push them out of Mali. Although the Libyan government is obviously in no position to investigate and confirm that AQIM or its sympathizers were the source of these attacks, they were nevertheless an ominous sign of an expanding terrorist area of operations.

Although there were no attacks on the scale of Benghazi attacks, retributive killings against former regime officials as well as car bombings and other attacks on representatives and symbols of Libya's new government continued throughout 2013. More recently, al Qaeda–linked groups that France chased out of Mali in 2013 have been reported in southern Libya, prompting the French chief of defense Admiral Edourd Guillaud to raise the possibility of international military action in early 2014.[52]

Jihadists are by no means the only source of violence and have surely not taken over the country, but they remain a serious problem and possible future threat. Libya's vast expanses, porous borders, and widespread availability of weapons provide a good culture for future jihadist expansion and will continue to do so as long as the Libyan state is unable to bring its territory, and the east in particular, under control.

---

[52] Nicolas Champeaux, "Le Sud de la Libye, Nouveau Sanctuaire des Jihadistes" *RFI*, February 5, 2014.

Box 2.1: Major Armed Groups in Libya

Although many groups remain murky, some of the larger groups and groupings deserve special mention, given their importance to political and security developments.

The Zintan Military Council

One of the most powerful and well-organized groups in Libya, the brigades under this grouping played an integral part in the rebel capture of Tripoli in August 2011, which gives them a certain degree of legitimacy. They are also the captors of Saif Al-Islam, which further strengthens their position. One of their leaders, Osama al-Juwaili, was appointed minister of defense shortly after the war by the NTC—reportedly under significant pressure. The Zintanis occupied

Tanks in a heavy weapons depot in Zintan, Tripolitania, Libya, July 10, 2012 (Marco Salustro/Corbis/APImages).

RAND RR577-2.3

the Tripoli airport for several months, and (like several other groups) are rumored to be involved in smuggling and other illegal activities.[1]

Estimated at 4,000 strong, the Zintanis have clashed on more than one occasion with Islamist-aligned militias in Tripoli, where both groups continue to maintain a significant presence.[2] The Zintanis are linked closely to brigades such as the Al Qaqaa brigade, which was one of the first to enter Tripoli and has intervened in various clashes there since the end of the war. The Al Qaqaa brigade is one of the main brigades controlling western Tripoli and is perceived to be linked to the National Forces Alliance (NFA), Libya's main moderate political coalition (see Chapter Three).

Misrata Brigades

Misrata is Zintan's main competitor for power and influence in Libya. As noted earlier, Misrata was one of the few rebel-held areas outside the east during the first months of the war, and was besieged by Qaddafi forces. Its population suffered enormously as a result. Fighters from Misrata not only despised the regime, they also felt they had a special claim to the mantle of national leadership once the war was over, given what they had endured. The Misratan brigades sometimes align with the Muslim Brotherhood and its political party, the Justice and Cooperation Party (JCP). Many are part of the LSF and thus officially report to the government, even though they take orders from it at their own volition.

Souk al Jouma and Sadun al-Suwayli Brigades

The Souk al Jouma Brigade has controlled Mitiga airport and munitions stored nearby and is linked to the wartime Islamist military leader Hakim Belhaj. The Sadun al-Suwayli Brigade had the honor of leading the final attack on Sirte, in which Qaddafi was killed, and was

---

[1] Omar Ashour, "Libyan Islamists Unpacked," *Brookings Doha Center Policy Briefing*, May 2012; Dario Cristiani, *The Zintan Militia and the Fragmented Libyan State*, Washington, D.C.: Jamestown Foundation, January 2012; Ezzeldeen Khalil, "Minding the Militias," *Janes Intelligence Review*, January 17, 2013.

[2] "Guide to Libya's Militias," *BBC Online*, September 28, 2012.

later accused of kidnapping a journalist who had criticized Misrata.[3] According to one report, Misrata's brigades control more than 820 tanks, dozens of heavy artillery pieces, and more than 2,300 vehicles equipped with machine guns and anti-aircraft weapons.[4]

February 17 Brigade

The February 17 Brigade is another powerful Islamist group in the east, comprised of 12 different brigades with membership estimated between 1,500 and 3,000 and significant stores of heavy weapons. It has served as a government force for operations in Kufra and elsewhere in Libya. It is financed by the Ministry of Defense. Notably, this was the group responsible for the protection of the U.S. diplomatic compound in Benghazi prior to the attack on September 11, 2012. Its leader, Fawzi Bukatif, is in fact from a Misratan family, and has close ties to Ismail al-Sallabi of Rafallah al-Sahati and other powerful Islamists in the region.[5]

Libyan Shield 1

Important branches of LSF exist nationwide, including in Misrata and Zawia. A key force in the east, however, is Libyan Shield 1, led by a man named Wisam bin Hamid. Despite being part of the LSF, bin Hamid has openly scoffed at Tripoli's orders and effectively runs his own operation. Hamid is an Islamist conservative, with possible jihadist sympathies.[6] His brigade has been accused of torturing Coptic Christians in a secret prison in Benghazi, and was implicated in the deaths of protesters during the violence in Benghazi in June

---

[3] "Guide to Libya's Militias," 2012.

[4] Brian McQuinn, "Armed Groups in Libya: Typology and Roles," *Small Arms Survey*, No. 18, June 2012a.

[5] "Guide to Libya's Militias," 2012; "Unity Under Strain," *Africa Confidential*, Vol. 53, No. 25, December 14, 2012.

[6] *Al Qaeda in Libya: A Profile*, Federal Research Division, Library of Congress, August 2012.

2013, and his house was later burned, likely in retribution for the assassination of a popular security officer.[7]

Ansar al-Sharia (Benghazi)

The group most closely associated with the Benghazi attack goes by the name Ansar al-Sharia (AAS-B). An Islamist group with possible jihadists among it, AAS-B has engaged in public service and charitable projects, including welfare support, cleaning and repairing roads, providing security for the Jala'a hospital, and distributing alms during Ramadan. In the absence of the state, this strategy has helped it gain some acceptance with the Benghazi public, despite the outcry against it in the aftermath of the attacks and its ultra-conservative views, which led it to reject the authority of the democratic political process altogether. Its leader is Muhammed Ali al-Zahawi, who fought with Rafallah al Sahati in Misrata during the war.[8]

Abu Salim Martyrs Brigade

Located in Derna, east of Benghazi, the Abu Salim Martyrs Brigade is a militant Islamist group with roots in the LIFG, which struggled against the Qaddafi regime for two decades prior to his overthrow. Led by Salim Derbi, it attempted to proclaim *shari'a* in Derna in 2012 after having reportedly assassinated Muhammed al-Hasi, the man in charge of internal security in Derna for the national government. It was assigned to the SSC, but was also reported to have sought closer ties with AQIM.[9]

---

[7] Andrew Engel, "A Way Forward in Benghazi," Washington Institute for Near East Policy, *PolicyWatch* 2088, June 12, 2013.

[8] Allison Pargeter, "Islamist Militant Groups in Post-Qadhafi Libya, " CTC Sentinel, Vol. 6, No. 2, February 2013; Frederic Wehrey, "The Struggle for Security in Eastern Libya," Carnegie Endowment, September 19, 2012; Isabelle Mandraud, "Poussée de fièvre à Benghazi contre le journal satirique [High Fever in Benghazi Against the Satirical Newspaper]," *Le Monde*, September 20, 2012.

[9] Wehrey, 2012b; Con Coughlin, "Al Qaeda in the Age of Obama," *Wall Street Journal*, December 7, 2012.

Ansar al-Sharia (Derna)

Sometimes described as a radical offshoot of the Abu Salim Martyrs Brigade, Ansar al-Sharia in Derna (AAS-D) is not formally connected with the Benghazi group of the same name, but shares many of the same ideals. (Ansar al Sharia, which means defenders of *shari'a*, is an increasingly common name for a new generation of militant Islamic groups and has been used also in nearby Tunisia as well as by groups affiliated with al Qaeda in the Arabian Peninsula.) It is led by a man named Sufian Bin Qumu, who was an inmate at the U.S. detention facility in Guantanamo Bay, and once served as a driver for Osama bin Laden. Bin Qumu has been described as incompetent, but he appears to have helped ensure that Derna has become a magnet for jihadists from Libya and elsewhere. He is widely reported to be running a training camp for approximately 200 jihadists in the forest outside of town.[10]

Libya Revolutionaries Operations Room

Initially set up by Libyan congress head Nouri Abu Sahmaine to protect and secure Tripoli in August 2013, this organization was responsible for kidnapping Prime Minister Zeidan in October of that year. The Tripoli branch was stripped of its mandate, but a partner branch was later opened in Benghazi with similar objectives.

---

[10] Daniel Nisman, "The Jihadist Gateway to Africa," *Wall Street Journal*, January 21, 2013.

CHAPTER THREE

Statebuilding Challenges

From a certain perspective, expanding violence in Libya was a direct consequence of the weakness of the Libyan state, which lacked sovereignty in the classical sense that it did not have a legitimate monopoly on the use of force within its territory. Libya's basic statebuilding needs were, and remain, significant. The conditions under which these needs had to be met were also very challenging.

On a fundamental level, Libya had to determine what its political system would be, so that the tensions that existed between social forces in the country could be resolved through a political process rather than violence. It also had to strengthen administrative institutions—the ministries, agencies, and other bodies of the state—so that they could provide a minimum of governance. These institutions were in a state of disarray after four decades of dictatorship and a war that had led to the ouster of many Qaddafi-era functionaries and their replacement with revolutionaries, although their weakness was partially concealed by Libya's energy wealth.

Even under the best conditions, building political and administrative institutions would be difficult. The challenge was hugely compounded, however, by the basic political weakness of the Libyan authorities, widespread insecurity, and the limited international role. As a result, the process soon fell behind the ambitious timeline Libyans had established for statebuilding during the war, creating further frustration among the populace.

The NTC's main focus during the war was overthrowing Qaddafi, but, under pressure from its international benefactors, it did lay out a basic framework for post-conflict Libyan politics. A declaration on August 3, 2011, delineated its authorities and outlined a roadmap for transition to elected institutions and constitutional government. The NTC was to hand over power within a year of formally declaring the country liberated from Qaddafi's rule. It would have 90 days to write an electoral law, appoint an electoral commission, and call elections for a national constituent assembly. These elections were to be held within 240 days of liberation.

Importantly, the primary responsibility of the constituent assembly was to nominate a committee to draft the new constitution. It was given 30 days to do this and the committee itself was given 60 more days for its work, after which the constitution would be put up for a national referendum. If it passed, elections of Libya's first constitutional government would follow. In the interim, the NTC and its successor would exercise both executive and legislative authority, operating effectively as a caretaker government.

Based on the experience of constitution writing in other transitioning states, this was an ambitious timeline.[1] It proved impossible to uphold.

The National Transitional Council

The first problem was the political weakness of the NTC, which led the country in the immediate postwar period. The NTC had been established to represent the rebels on the international stage and manage the war effort itself. When Tripoli fell, it became the de facto transitional government of Libya and moved its operations from Benghazi to the capital. An interim government was established on November 24 under Prime Minister Abdul Raheem Al-Keeb and remained in place until elections could be held and a new government could be formed.

Despite its leadership during the war, the NTC was very weak. It lacked legitimacy, in part because it had not been sanctioned by elec-

---

[1] Laurel Miller, ed., *Framing the State in Times of Transition: Case Studies in Constitution Making*, Washington, D.C.: U.S. Institute of Peace, 2010.

tions. It was also not as representative of the forces on the ground as it might have been. Although it had broadened its membership to include representation from outside its original Benghazi base, the real war heroes were not the rebel political leaders but the military leaders. The fact that many NTC leaders were either expatriates who had fled the regime in the 1980s or recent regime officials who had defected early in the revolt also worked against the council's authority.

Moreover, it was internally divided, in part on account of the very efforts that had been made to broaden its representation. The divisions were symbolized by the differences between 'Abd al-Jalil, initially the head of NTC, and Mahmoud Jibril, head of its executive council. Jibril was the face of the NTC to the outside world, but had less sway in Libya than his titular role as de facto prime minister would indicate. The two of them never agreed on a division of labor and the division between the two positions would persist not only through the Al-Keeb period, but also beyond it, as discussed below.

The NTC leadership was both aware of these shortcomings and concerned that introducing controversial policies would further erode confidence in it. Leaders were also worried that decisions regarding the future of the country needed to be made by elected leaders. The result was a very slow and cautious overall approach to dealing with the country's post-conflict problems that frequently frustrated international officials who aimed to support the transition.[2]

The Federalist Challenge

In addition to the outbreaks of violence explained in Chapter Two, the NTC also faced a growing challenge from longstanding federalist forces in the east. In the 19th century, eastern Arab tribes had been brought together under the leadership of a conservative Sufi order led by the Senussi family. These tribes fought bitterly against Italian Fascist rule in the interwar period, eventually aligning with Allied forces against Mussolini during World War II. When Libya was granted

---

2   Interviews with U.S. and European officials, October 2, 2012.

independence in 1951, the Senussi monarch took control of the country and ruled through a loose confederal constitution. Qaddafi's 1969 coup was thus a direct overthrow of eastern, Senussi power. He acted harshly against the former leaders and their allied tribes, moving government offices, including the national oil corporation, to Tripoli, and taking other measures to repress regional powers. Economic and social conditions in Benghazi lagged behind Tripoli, a fact that was particularly aggravating to easterners because some 80 percent of Libya's oil wealth is located in the eastern Sirte Basin.[3]

Given this history, it is unsurprising that the revolt against Qaddafi started in the east. It is also unsurprising that the NTC's composition had been heavily tilted toward the region in the early stages of the war, given the war's origins in Benghazi. As the war progressed, however, the NTC came to include prominent expatriates with western roots. After the war, the NTC moved to Tripoli and some easterners grew concerned that they were losing influence over the revolution and that Tripoli's past neglect of Cyrenaica might continue.

Tensions flared in March 2012 when the NTC announced its plan to allocate 60 seats in the national assembly to the east, and over 100 to the west. The decision was justified on the grounds that the west was more populous than the east, but easterners nevertheless felt that the cards were being stacked against them. As a result, a group known as the Barqa Council declared itself to be the interim government of Cyrenaica (*Barqa* is the Arabic word for the province) and called for a boycott of the upcoming parliamentary elections. The Council's members numbered in the thousands and came from a variety of tribes, ex-revolutionaries, and other groups.

It is important to note that the Barqa Council's objective was not to secede altogether from Libya. They sought greater autonomy in a region that would have its own parliament, police, courts, and a capital in Benghazi. At the same time, however, they acknowledged that

---

[3]   Akbar Ahmed and Frankie Martin, "Understanding the Sanusi of Cyrenaica," Al Jazeera. com, March 26, 2012; Wehrey, 2012b. See also E. E. Evans-Pritchard, *The Sanusi of Cyrenaica*, Oxford, UK: Oxford University Press, 1954.

control over some issues, including foreign and defense policy and the distribution of oil revenues, should remain with Tripoli.

Concern nevertheless grew both in Libya and internationally that the east was headed toward secession, and with it, Libya toward renewed fighting. "This is very dangerous. This is a blatant call for fragmentation," said one member of the NTC.[4] It did not help that the Barqa Council was backed by an estimated 61 eastern militias that together made up a so-called Barqa Army, which proceeded to establish roadblocks at the main crossing point between east and west, seriously hampering travel between the two regions.[5]

As the election approached, Barqa supporters attacked election offices in Benghazi. As with so many developments in Libya, and especially the east, it was unclear to what extent these moves were ordered by the leadership of the Barqa Council, to what extent they were condoned, and to what extent they were simply spontaneous expressions of frustration by the people. Whatever their cause, these attacks sparked a backlash. Several local militias intervened, arresting the attackers. Public protests against the council followed. Recognizing that they were doing more harm than good for their cause, the Barqa Council leadership backed down from its position and dismantled its roadblock.[6]

The issues that underlay the appeal of the federalists, however— fear of neglect by Tripoli and frustration with the overall pace of post-revolutionary progress—would persist and the federalist movement would evolve over time, growing even more problematic in 2013, when a version of it took much of the energy infrastructure in the east hostage.

Many easterners resent Tripoli's control over energy decisions, especially given that the basin with the largest reserves, the Sirte Basin, is located largely in the east (see Figure 4.2 in Chapter Four). In an effort to quell discontent and respond to the demands of the federalists,

---

[4] "Libya Tribal Leaders Break Away from Interim Government," Associated Press, March 6, 2012.

[5] Rami Al-Shaheibi, "Eastern Libya Pulls Away from Central Government," Associated Press, March 6, 2012.

[6] Wehrey, 2012b.

the Libyan government announced that it would move the offices of the National Oil Corporation (NOC) to Benghazi, along with Libyan Airlines, the Libya Company for Insurance, and the Internal Investment Company.[7] (The NOC had been based in Benghazi prior to 1973.) There has been no serious move, however, to actually implement this, prompting further resentment.

Despite this effort at reconciliation, militias in the east and the west took Libya's oil production hostage in August 2013. The eastern port terminals of Es Sider, Ras Lanuf, Brega, and Hariga were all shut down by strikes in which workers demanded higher wages, more regional independence, and a larger share of Libya's national oil revenues. Meanwhile, in the west, powerful Zintani militia shut down pipelines connecting the El Feel and El Sharara fields to terminals in Mellitah and Zawiya in response.[8]

The groups that shut down the oil ports were members of the Oil Facilities Guard and followers of Ibrahim Jedhran, a federalist leader of the Cyrenaican Transitional Council. They have refused to lift their siege unless the government implements their federalist demands and have threatened to sell oil independently of the state.

Challenges to General National Congress

The 2012 tensions created by the eastern federalists were linked to the ongoing effort to hold national elections that would replace the NTC with an interim parliament called the General National Congress (GNC). In addition to being a good in themselves, elections were intended to provide Libya with a stronger, more legitimate government than the NTC. Many international observers and members of the government hoped the elections would empower a government with a pop-

[7]   Ahmed Ruhayem, "Federalists Celebrate Return of NOC to Benghazi," *Libya Herald*, June 7, 2013.

[8]   Suleiman Al-Khalidi and Julia Payne, "Update 2-Libya Struggles to Resume Oil Exports," Reuters, September 16, 2013.

ular mandate to resolve contentious issues hanging over the transition process.

Held on July 7, 2012, in the face of considerable skepticism about their feasibility, the elections became the bright spot in the international postwar effort. UNSMIL and nongovernmental organizations like the International Foundation for Electoral Systems (IFES) worked with the Libyan electoral commission to register voters, design and implement an electoral formula, and stage the polls. There were some issues with administration and small irregularities, but the international community judged the elections free and fair. More importantly, over 80 percent of Libyans believe the vote was either "completely free and fair" or somewhat "free and fair."[9]

On a technical and symbolic level the elections were a clear success. After 42 years of authoritarian rule, there were doubts as to whether Libyans would embrace participatory politics. The election turnout—estimated at 60 percent—exceeded expectations, indicating that the population was engaged and enthusiastic about democracy. The fact that they were largely free of violence also suggested that the majority of Libyans supported a peaceful transition.

On a political level, however, the elections did not create a stronger government. The new parliament was highly fragmented due to the absence of organized political parties that could aggregate interests nationwide. Moreover, because there were so many candidates and no second round of voting, many of the independents elected actually had less than 20 percent of vote in their own districts.[10] Initial judgments that the moderates had won a clear victory soon proved overstated, given the strength of conservative Islamists not aligned with any party. The result was a broad-based congress, but one in which there was a high degree of parochialism and an extremely wide variety of agendas.

Given this diversity, it proved very difficult to form a government. Mustafa Abu Shagur, who was nominated prime minister at the outset,

---

[9] National Democratic Institute, "Believing in Democracy: Public Opinion Survey in Libya," August 2013a.

[10] Wolfram Lacher, "Fault Lines of the Revolution: Political Actors, Camps, and Conflicts in the New Libya," SWP Research Paper, May 2013.

failed twice. (He argues that this was in part because he was unwilling to accept candidates for ministerial positions for purely political reasons.)[11] He finally ceded his post to Ali Zeidan, who rejected Shagur's technocratic approach and accepted that ministerial and other positions would need to be shared among various groups if the government was to stand.

Zeidan offered each of the two major political groupings in the GNC, the NFA and the JCP, five cabinet posts. He also spread out representation among Libya's different regions. To avoid hewing too closely to a strategy of co-optation and patronage politics, Zeidan appointed independents to head the cabinet positions that Libyans refer to as the "sovereign posts," which encompass Defense, Interior, Foreign Affairs, Justice, Finance, and International Cooperation. This formula elicited enough support to win approval from the GNC but created tensions within the government and diminished Zeidan's ability to control his cabinet. The contentious and drawn-out process meanwhile squandered positive momentum from the July 7 election.

The GNC also elected a president of the assembly, Mohamed al-Magariaf. Magariaf operated as if he were Libya's head of state, but the authorities of his position and its relationship with Zeidan's government were not at all clear. Magariaf took on the role of commander in chief and frequently represented Libya at international fora, such as the UN General Assembly meeting held in New York in September 2012.

To his admirers, Magariaf was a strong and decisive leader who proved his revolutionary credentials through his participation in the historic opposition group, the National Front for the Salvation of Libya. To his critics, however, he was domineering, authoritarian in his management style, and constantly overstepping his authority.

These internal divisions and contradictions made it difficult for the GNC to govern. The assembly soon found itself at the mercy of a restive street, however, and embroiled in debate over a lustration law, known as the political isolation law, that reached a crisis pitch in the first half of 2013. Although some form of lustration is normal in a post-conflict situation, in Libya, as in Iraq, the matter went too far and

---

[11] Interview, Tripoli, February 3, 2013.

In this February 17, 2013, photo, Libyan interim President Mohamad al-Magariaf flashes the victory sign to crowds during the celebration of the second anniversary of the Libyan revolution in Benghazi, Libya. Libya's parliament passed a law on May 5, 2013, that bans officials who held senior positions under ousted dictator Moammar Qaddafi from holding high-level government posts, a move that could disqualify much of the country's political elite from office, including Magariaf (AP Photo/Mohammad Hannon).

RAND RR577-3.1

Box 3.1: The Role of the Exile Community

Exiles from the Qaddafi regime have played a significant, although sometimes controversial, role in Libya's transition. This includes self-exiles, who were primarily motivated to seek a better life, as well as committed oppositionists who fled after failed bids to overthrow the regime. Many of the exiles in this latter camp were members of the National Front for the Salvation of Libya, which operated as an umbrella group for opponents of the Qaddafi regime, many of different ideological persuasions. Some of these individuals, now in their 60s, have returned to Libya after several decades in exile.[1] This common profile matches several of the key figures in Libya's political

---

[1] At 72, Magariaf is about a decade older than the others cited in this paragraph.

transition, including former President Mohamed al-Magariaf, Prime Minister Ali Zeidan, Prime Minister nominee and former Deputy Prime Minister Mustafa Abu Shagur, former Prime Minister Abdul Raheem al-Keeb, and former Oil Minister 'Ali Tarhouni. These individuals tend to be highly educated. For example, Shagur, Tarhouni, and al-Keeb all hold Ph.D.'s and had careers as accomplished academics at U.S. universities. As for Magariaf and Zeidan, they worked as Libyan diplomats before turning against the Qaddafi regime. This wonkish profile is not confined to just the upper echelon of Libya's new political leadership. Several members of the GNC, such as the recently resigned Hassan al-Amin, were longtime exiles in the UK and the United States. In Zeidan's cabinet, 11 of 30 ministers have advanced degrees from Western universities.[2] Magariaf's replacement, Abu Sahmayn, also studied in the UK. These individuals are sometimes jokingly referred to by other Libyans as "dual SIM cards," in reference to their practice of switching out SIM cards in their mobile phones as they jet from one location to another.

The Libyan exile community bucks the typical situation in which the community's Achilles heel is its susceptibility to the charge of dual loyalties. In postwar Iraq, where exiled politicians played a similarly prominent role, this community was frequently derided as a fifth column of foreign influence. For example, Nuri al-Maliki and Abdel Aziz al-Hakim were often portrayed by their critics as puppets of Iran. On the other side, Iyad Allawi was seen as a favorite of Turkey and Tariq al-Hashimi as close to Saudi Arabia. In the case of Libya, the exile community did not return with the same level of baggage as their Iraqi counterparts. This is because, in the Iraq case, the allegation of dual loyalties was reinforced by the fact that the exiles shared a common sectarian identity with their purported patrons. Al-Maliki and al-Hakim are Shi'a, while Allawi and Hashimi are Sunni.

The weakness of Magariaf, Zeidan, Shagur, and others is not so much that they are viewed as stooges of the West, but that they are

---

2   Short biographies of the ministers in the Zeidan cabinet are available, in Arabic, from the National Center for the Support of Decision-Making.

less familiar with present realities in Libya and they lack strong ties to the country's new power brokers. Exiles were empowered by the February 17th Revolution but were not on the ground at its outset. They only belatedly have come to know the militia leaders and local councils that sprung up to organize and prosecute the opposition against the regime.

Many of the exiles were also academics with little experience as political operators. Few doubt the good intentions or analytical skills of an individual like Al-Keeb, but he was a relative neophyte in the world of politics. Similarly, when Shagur was later elected as the GNC's first choice for prime minister, he twice attempted to form technocratic governments rather than divvying up the ministries among the major political and tribal factions.[3] Shagur's unwillingness to play power politics was high-minded but ultimately ineffective, and he lost a no-confidence vote.

---

[3] Interview with Shagur, Tripoli, February 5, 2013.

became a means by which (primarily) conservative Islamist groups, whose leaders had not been tainted by association with the Qaddafi regime, sought to strengthen their political hand against the moderates.

Both the process by which the law was negotiated and its content damaged the legitimacy of the government and raised concerns about the commitment of some groups to a peaceful transition. The law, which was eventually passed in May 2013 as Law #13, pitted the GNC's largest coalition bloc, the NFA, against the JCP. The NFA is headed by the most prominent holdover from the Qaddafi-era, Mahmoud Jibril, who held several high-ranking positions in the Qaddafi regime and thus had a particular interest in ensuring leniency in the law.

In addition to particular party interests, the law elicited strong feelings among the general public. Polling shows that a large majority of Libyans supported the exclusion of high-ranking officials of the Qaddafi era from public life. For example, in a 1,200-person poll conducted in early 2013, 64 percent of respondents urged passage of a political isolation law that would encompass those that held "leadership positions" under Qaddafi.[12] This was in contrast to only 18 percent of respondents who opposed such a law. In another poll conducted by the National Democratic Institute, 69 percent favored some form of political exclusion.[13]

Among the minority that had reservations about the law were many elite expatriates who recognized the damage the law could do if it banished much-needed technocratic expertise or led to a violent backlash from groups that had served the regime. In particular, there was also a risk that overzealous legislation would create fissures between the new state and the communities that had benefited from Qaddafi's rule, such as Sirte, Bani Walid, Tawergha, and Ghat, and thereby create further risk of strife. Meanwhile, a more lenient law would also facilitate the return of exiles from neighboring Egypt and Tunisia.

In the end, the public debate took a backseat to the strong-arm tactics of some former revolutionaries (*thuwwar*), who strongly opposed the participation of what they classify as the "dregs" of the former regime in the new political order. They surrounded government ministries, shut down the GNC itself, and threatened the safety of the prime minister.[14] This ultimately intimidated the GNC into passing a draconian version of the law. Despite the fact that many GNC members privately voiced reservations about the law, when it came time to vote, 164 members approved the bill, with only four abstaining and no member opposing it.[15] To put into perspective the pressure GNC members felt, even those who were ultimately subject to the law's exclusions, such as Magariaf (who once served as Ambassador to India), felt compelled to publicly support it.

---

[12] Al-Manara, "Istitlāʿ lil Rāʾī Yuzhir Anna Akthar min 64% min Istatalaʿat Arāʿihim maʿ Qānūn al-ʿAzl al-Siyāsī fī Lībīya [An Opinion Poll Shows That More Than 64% of Those Polled Are for the Political Isolation Law in Libya]," March 7, 2013.

[13] National Democratic Institute, 2013a.

[14] Hadi Fornaji, "Blockades Polarizing Libya; Militiamen Now Hit Electricity Ministry," *Libya Herald*, May 2, 2013.

[15] GNC, "Al-Muʾtamar al-Watanī al-ʿĀmm Yuqirr Qānūn al-ʿAzl al-Siyāsī [The GNC Approves the Political Isolation Law]," May 5, 2013.

In this November 1, 2012, photo, young men representing ex-revolutionary militia groups, arriving from different towns in Libya, gather in front of the GNC building in Tripoli, Libya. A few days before, armed protestors cut the main road leading to the Parliament and vowed not to leave until members of the ousted Qaddafi regime were excluded from political life. Five of the 27 ministers would be reconsidered, a spokesman said, after concerns were raised over their ties to the deposed regime. But that was not good enough for the protesters, who tried to storm the building but were turned back by security forces (AP Photo/Gaia Anderson).
RAND *RR577-3.2*

The passage of the political isolation law forced the removal of several senior officials, including the president and deputy president of the GNC and the Interior Minister.[16] An independent body, the Public Officials Standards Commission,[17] was established to carry out the provisions of the law, but the need for enforcement has been somewhat obviated by voluntary resignations (e.g., Magariaf, Jum'a Atiga, 'Ashour Shuweil). The result is the loss of some of Libya's most expe-

---

[16] Full Arabic-language text of the political isolation law can be accessed from the GNC's website.

[17] This unwieldy name comes from the Arabic, Hay'at Tatbīq Ma'āyīr Tawalī al-Manāsib al-'Amma.

eaucrats and a consequent reduction in already weak insti-
ιpacity. Also, because it disqualifies any military officer who
ded forces under Qaddafi from public office, it seriously com-
plica. already stalled security sector reform efforts. Finally, the passage of the law strengthened the hand of the Islamists.

Constitutional Challenges

The weakness of the NTC; the need to hold elections; the difficulties
encountered in forming a government after the GNC was elected; the
divisions within that body; the row over the political isolation law; and,
above all, the consistently unstable security situation, which greatly
impeded the working of Libya's transitional state, stalled Libya's progress toward establishing a constitution. Although the elections of the
GNC were held according to the schedule set out during the war, serious setbacks soon arose.

The biggest stumbling block has been the question of how the
constitutional drafting committee would be established—specifically,
whether it would be a body appointed by the GNC or whether it would
be elected directly by the people. Originally, the committee was to be
appointed, but the NTC, under pressure from the federalists, changed
its position at the end of its term, backing direct election instead.[18] A
subsequent decision by the Libyan courts annulled the NTC's about-
face, but the question remained open, and, on April 10, 2013, the GNC
voted in favor of direct election.

The GNC's main role in drafting a constitution thus became
passing the electoral law that would enable elections of the drafting
committee. In July, the GNC finally approved the law, and elections
for the drafting committee were expected in early 2014.

The actual drafting of the constitution thus still lies ahead. It will
inevitably raise a number of hot issues, including determining the role

---

[18] Karim Mezran and Duncan Pickard, "Libya's Constitutional Process: Moving Forward?"
The Atlantic Council, April 13, 2013.

of religion in the state and the balance of political power between the central government and local administrators.

On the issue of identity, Libyans are likely to adopt similar language as their counterparts in Egypt and Tunisia, whose post-revolution constitutions reaffirm the states' Arab-Islamic identity.[19] More vexing, however, will be how Libyans deal with minority-language rights. The vast majority of Libyans are Arabs or Arabicized Amizigh (Berber). But there is still a sizeable Amazigh community in Libya that has held on to Tamazight as their mother tongue. In addition, there is a small Tebu population that speaks in local dialects. Whether these communities are granted language rights will be an important indication of the inclusiveness of the state's ethnic identity.

Another issue is likely to be the role of Islamic law in the legal code. Libya is 97 percent Sunni Muslim, but there is variance among the groups about how important Islam should be in the society.[20] Although many Libyans view their country as moderately Islamic, polling after the war indicated a strong conservative streak. Most Libyans believe the political system should be shaped by Islam, although they differ in their views of what this means. For example, the majority of men and women (81 percent) believe that women should wear the Hijab and most of these believe the state should encourage women to do so.[21] Within these parameters, however, there was significant room for divergence.

Like its neighbors, Libya will almost certainly opt for an overt mention of *shari'a* in its constitution. This should not be viewed as a foreboding sign in the West. Even in secular-leaning states with

---

[19] Article One of Egypt's Constitution states "The Egyptian people are a part of the Arab and Islamic communities." At the time of this writing, Tunisia has yet to produce a final version of its constitution, but Article 1 of the latest draft (dated from December 2012) states that "Islam is [Tunisia's] religion and Arabic is its language."

[20] Central Intelligence Agency, "Africa: Libya," *The World Factbook*, 2013.

[21] Megan Doherty, "Building a New Libya: Citizen Views on Libya's Electoral and Political Process," National Democratic Institute, May 2012a; Megan Doherty, "Give Us Change We Can See: Citizen Views on Libya's Political Process," National Democratic Institute, December 2012b; National Democratic Institute, 2013a.

Muslim-majority populations, it is common to identify *shari'a* as a source, and sometimes as *the* source,[22] of legislation.

What is more important is how *shari'a* is defined—in other words, is it restricted to a narrow corpus of Islamic law or is it defined broadly? The second important consideration is whether the constitution identifies a body to vet legislation based on its conformity to Islamic law. The third and final issue related to *shari'a* is how its rulings are incorporated into family law. Even in Muslim-majority states operating under a civil code, family law is often governed by Islamic rulings on marriage rights, inheritance, child custody, and so forth. In Libya, the fidelity of family law with *shari'a* is likely to be a marker issue on which some drafters may try to "out-Islamist" their less doctrinal counterparts.

Even more so than minority rights and *shari'a*, the scope of federal power is the biggest landmine facing Libya's constitution drafters. Libya watchers were once quick to note that the July 2012 elections settled the federalism debate. The election turnout may have been a strong indicator that Libyans want a unified state, but it hardly settled the question of how much power Libyans want aggregated in the hands of the central government. The fact that the Committee of 60 will be comprised of 20 drafters drawn from each of Libya's three main regions—the same formula that was used to write the 1951 constitution—is more evidence of the continued sensitivity of regional issues.

The degree of decentralization that Libya's constitution drafters ultimately adopt remains an open question, but the debates will likely focus on several interrelated issues. The first is the scope of federal control over the country's investment budget. Those that favor centralization are likely to advocate for federal control of budgets; perhaps placating opponents by conceding a reference to Libyans' equal entitlement to state resources. Whereas Libyans from historically marginalized regions, and those from the east in particular, may advocate for enshrining a fixed allocation of state spending on a region-by-region basis—as is the case in the Kurdistan Region of Iraq today. Similarly,

---

[22] In Egypt's constitution, *shari'a* is identified as the principal source of legislation. This was the case before the January 25th Revolution and the wording remains the same after the constitution was rewritten in 2012.

there will almost certainly be debates over who exercises control over security forces. Advocates for a strong center are likely to argue that the state must exercise strict control over all security organs. There will be others, however, that see local security forces as a guarantor against the return of an authoritarian state.

Political Outlook

By the end of 2013, disaffection with the GNC had become widespread, and formal politics in Libya was becoming less and less relevant. The two major groups in parliament had failed to reach political compromises on the big issues and opted to use boycotts (or the threat of boycotts) rather than engage in real debate. This gave the impression that the GNC's major political parties were simply posturing for the next elections.[23]

The GNC lacks credibility as a result of having overstepped its mandate on the one hand, and accomplished little on the other. It is telling that all three of the GNC members interviewed for this study conceded that the assembly was held in such low esteem by the public that it would not be possible for the body to select the "Committee of 60" that will draft Libya's constitution. Rather, the interviewees supported direct election of the drafters to avoid the taint that would come from their association with the GNC, should the GNC select them as initially conceived by the NTC.

The mandate of the GNC expired in February 2014. At the time of this writing, it had issued a very controversial decision extending its mandate until the end of 2014. In a state in which militias are becoming more entrenched, where insecurity persists, and where the state exercises little control in entire regions of the country, the relevance of the formal political process has been questioned by many observers. The real power brokers in post-Qaddafi Libya are the militias that control key strategic transit points, self-anointed clerics that challenge the

---

[23] Interview with Libyan analyst in Tripoli, February 1, 2013; interview with Libyan politician in Tripoli, February 3, 2013.

Mufti's religious authority, and tribal leaders nationwide. The democratic political process that many Libyans believed they were fighting for, in other words, is dangerously stalled. Some of the steps that might be taken to get it back on track are outlined in Chapter Six, but it will not happen overnight.

CHAPTER FOUR

Economic Stabilization and the Oil Economy

Civil wars most frequently occur in states that lack the resources necessary to sustain the basic institutions of governance and provide public services. Libya, however, was wealthy in comparison with many other war-torn countries. Relatively high levels of per capita income made it look like a good candidate for an easy post-conflict transition, and economic activity was widely expected to return rapidly after the war. This, in turn, was expected to facilitate a stable transition to peace and lessen the financial burden on international donors. In theory, Libya should have been well placed to foot the bill for its own reconstruction. Wealth and a fairly well-educated population promised opportunities for productive employment that itself would facilitate rebel disarmament and reintegration.

Unfortunately, Libya's postwar economic recovery did not go according to plan, largely because of the stalled political process and lack of security. Oil production recovered quickly to near-prewar levels after the war, but mounting insecurity proved a major impediment to progress on other economic tasks. Violence distracted the government while scaring off foreign workers and investors, both of which were needed for successful economic stabilization. For a time, Libya was able to subsist reasonably well on oil revenues. Sadly, however, 18 months after Qaddafi's death, political turbulence—coupled with the weakness of the Libyan state—permitted gangs and militias to take control of multiple oil production facilities, driving oil production back down to dangerously low levels, thereby demonstrating how vulnerable the economy really was.

Libya's energy resources are both a blessing and a curse. On the one hand, they free Libya from some of the economic constraints other postwar countries face. They should also help encourage Europe, and to a lesser degree the United States, to stay invested in Libya's future, thereby slightly reducing the chances that Libya will utterly fall off Western policymakers' radars.

On the other hand, Libya's oil wealth has created problems— some unexpected, others predictable. If it decreases the need for foreign assistance, oil also makes it harder for international actors to influence Libyan politics. Aside from peacekeeping forces, the main lever the international community would normally have in a post-conflict situation is foreign aid, but aid is not a significant factor in Libya's case. Libya's relative wealth also obscured the underdevelopment and weakness of Libyan economic institutions and public administration. In the long term, Libya's dependence on hydrocarbons could become a challenge to stability, especially efforts at democratization, if conditions for private enterprise are not improved and the economy does not diversify.

Under the prevailing conditions this will be an uphill battle. The fragility of the Libyan government's hold on power has meant that most economic policies are aimed at shoring up power, while buying time and allegiance. This is understandable, but not a recipe for pro-growth reform.

The Contraction and Recovery of Libya's Oil Production

Economic activity contracted sharply during the war, with gross domestic product (GDP) for 2011 falling by 60 percent from the 2010 level. A large part of this drop was due to the fact that the production of oil fell from 1.77 million barrels per day to a mere 22,000. In addition, Libya faced international economic sanctions imposed by UN Security Council Resolution 1971 when the revolt first began in February. Progress had been made just prior to the end of the war in releasing some of those funds, but Libyan authorities were still unable to access all the funds that had been cut off. Access to foreign exchange was limited and the foreign workers who had fled the country left many posts vacant.[1]

Luckily, the economic damage due to the conflict was relatively minimal. Since the east was under rebel control from early on in the conflict, damage there was limited. Misrata and other towns did experience significant shelling during the fighting, but the loss of key infrastructure and manufacturing (minimal in Libya in any event) was not extensive. The holdout towns of Sirte and Bani Walid were more heavily damaged in the final weeks of the war, but while slow reconstruction there appears to have contributed to conflict, it did not itself prove a major impediment to national economic recovery. In part, the low levels of physical damage are due to the fact that NATO planners went to great lengths to ensure that Libya's hydrocarbon industry was not seriously disrupted by military operations.

Even though NATO avoided targeting Libyan infrastructure, oil production dropped precipitously as a result of the fighting on the ground (see Figure 4.1). Libya has 47.1 billion barrels in proven reserves, the largest quantity in Africa and among the ten largest globally (Figure 4.3 shows Libya's oil production compared to the ten largest producers). Libya also has substantial natural gas reserves.[2] Before the revolution, oil output was 1.77 million barrels per day, or approximately 2 percent of global output. This fell to a mere 22,000 barrels per day by July 2011.[3] Nearly all of Libya's production facilities (Figure 4.2) were shut down. Fortunately, immediately after the war, oil production surged back, increasing to 1.6 million barrels per day a year after Qaddafi's death.[4] Oil accounts for more than 70 percent of Libya's GDP, 95 percent of its export earnings, and some 90 percent of government

---

[1] Ralph Chami Ahmed Al-Darwish, Serhan Cevik, Joshua Charap, Susan George, Borja Gracia, Simon Gray, and Sailendra Pattanayak, *Libya Beyond the Revolution: Challenges and Opportunities*, Washington, D.C.: International Monetary Fund, 2012.

[2] U.S. Energy Information Administration, "Libya: Analysis," June 2012.

[3] Chami et al., 2012.

[4] U.S. Energy Information Administration, 2012.

Figure 4.1
Recovery and Decline of Libya's Daily Oil Production, 2010–2013

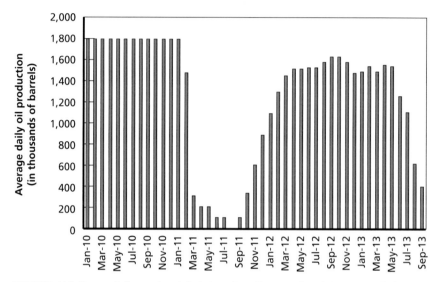

SOURCE: U.S. Energy Information Administration, "International Energy Statistics,"
data files on global oil production, 2013.
RAND RR577-4.1

revenue.[5] Given this dependence on hydrocarbons for current account
and fiscal balance, the rapid return of oil production was very important and may be acknowledged as a welcome success—though not one
that was particularly difficult to achieve.

The Oil "Curse" and Libya's Political Economic Challenges

If Libya's oil wealth offers benefits in its post-conflict reconstruction,
it also poses long-term risks, especially when it comes to building last-
ing democratic political institutions. When a country's oil wealth is
large and controlled by the state, there are significant incentives for
corruption and state capture by individual groups. In many cases, this

---

[5]   Chami et al., 2012; Mohsin Khan and Karim Mezran, "The Libyan Economy After the
Revolution: Still No Clear Vision," Atlantic Council Issue Brief, August 28, 2013.

Figure 4.2
Libya's Energy Infrastructure

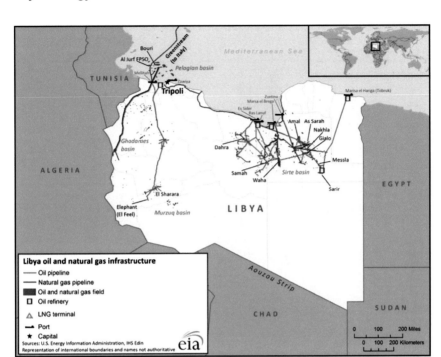

SOURCE: U.S. Energy Information Administration (September 2013).
NOTE: LNG = liquified natural gas.
RAND RR577-4.2

dynamic has contributed to the rise of authoritarianism or state collapse—what is sometimes known as the oil or resource curse.[6] Control
of oil has now become a factor in regional and other tensions.

The capture of oil facilities by militias in 2013 brought oil production to a postwar low of 160,000 barrels per day by September,
costing the Libyan government $130 million per day in lost revenue.[7]

---

[6] For a recent compendium on the subject, see Macartan Humphreys, Jeffrey D. Sachs, and
Joseph E. Stiglitz, *Escaping the Resource Curse,* New York: Columbia University Press, 2007.
See also Robert H. Bates, *When Things Fell Apart: State Failure in Late-Century Africa*, Cam-
bridge, UK: Cambridge University Press, 2008.

[7] Seraj Essul, "Oil Exports Down to 160,000 Barrels per Day: Oil Ministry," *Libya Herald,*
September 1, 2013; "Oil Strikes Cost Libya $130 Million per Day," UPI, September 13,
2011.

Figure 4.3
Libya Relative to the Top Ten Global Oil Producers, 2012

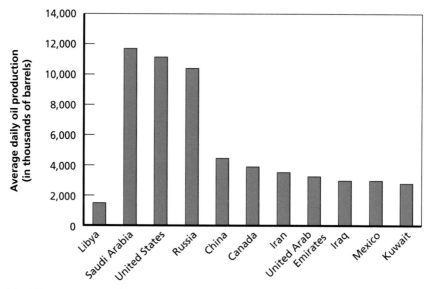

SOURCE: U.S. Energy Information Administration, 2013.
RAND *RR577-4.3*

Concern grew that the unrest might deter foreign firms from further investment in Libya's energy sector or even from buying oil from Libya in the future.[8] Prime Minister Zeidan promised to arrest the striking workers (who, in theory, worked for him) and restore production, but it was very unclear how he would do so without reliable security forces of his own.[9] The Zintanis ended their strike in September, but the strike in the east continued. This created major problems for European firms, such as Eni in particular, which relied on light crude imports from Libya for its refineries at home.[10]

---

[8]   Ajay Makan, "Libya and International Oil Groups Pay the Price for Unrest," *Financial Times*, September 16, 2011.

[9]   Clifford Krauss, "In Libya, Unrest Brings Oil Industry to Standstill," *The New York Times*, September 12, 2013.

[10]   Interview with U.S. official, December 17, 2013.

Libya's energy wealth also skews its labor market. Although per capita income is not on a scale commensurate with the Arab Gulf States, wages and expectations are relatively high; Libyans prefer to work for the government because expectations in the public sector are lower and wages higher. Moreover, the vast reservoir of workers willing to work at low wages from Egypt and sub-Saharan Africa makes private-sector jobs less attractive. Unless the government no longer provides employment, Libyans are unlikely to take them.

In the near term, oil wealth facilitates and complicates demobilization and disarmament efforts. Clearly, it is beneficial that the government has the capacity to pay salaries to former revolutionaries. Yet the tradition of well-paid state salaries has created unreasonably high expectations for employment among many rebels. If the government jobs that are offered to former rebels do not offer a substantial and appealing alternative form of identity, prestige, and social position, *thuwwar* are likely to remain unsatisfied. If the jobs are "ghost jobs" that pay a salary but do not require the employee to actually show up for work, giving them to former rebels could have the opposite of the intended effect, enabling rebels to remain a part of their militias longer than would be the case were if they had to find gainful employment elsewhere.

Managing Libya's Energy Wealth

Libya will need to manage its energy carefully.[11] Transparency in the collection and spending of its hydrocarbon wealth is particularly important. Like other developing countries, Libya will almost certainly keep its energy industry under state ownership. To protect against some of the inefficiencies that can arise from public ownership, however, the Libyan authorities might consider adding one or two highly regarded international businessmen or oil experts to the boards of directors of

---

[11] This subsection draws on Christopher S. Chivvis, Keith Crane, Peter Mandaville, and Jeffrey Martini, *Libya's Post Qaddafi Transition: The Nation-Building Challenge,* Santa Monica, Calif.: RAND Corporation, RR-129-SRF, November 2012.

the national energy companies. It will also be important to ensure that the National Oil Corporation (NOC) is allowed to retain enough revenue to ensure continued investment in the industry. To the extent possible, the NOC will want to collaborate with foreign corporations, although in doing so it will need to be careful to ensure full transparency, perhaps even going so far as to put the tender and bid process on national television—a practice that has been instituted in Iraq.

The question of how to distribute Libya's energy reserves is also thorny and has repercussions across the political spectrum. The preferred method, which is subsidies, needs to be reconsidered because it encourages Libyans to waste valuable resources that might be better spent on education, health care, and infrastructure development. Subsidies also create incentives to smuggle subsidized products, such as flour and gasoline, to neighboring states. Libya's subsidies are large; it will be a major challenge for future Libyan governments to reduce them without provoking a backlash.

The combination of subsidies and high public-sector wages drains resources for investment in other economic priorities and for Libya's future in general. One means of reigning in this spending would be to create separate accounts for different purposes. For example, one account might set aside money for current investment, another for future generations through a sovereign wealth fund, and a third for a rainy day fund in the event that world oil prices drop dramatically.

Libya's Economic Future

To sustain growth over the longer term, however, Libya will need economic reforms to improve the business environment. Although some reforms had begun prior to the war, Qaddafi's economic system was structured primarily to sustain his power, rather than for economic efficiency, and most post-Qaddafi policies will not help Libya move toward sustainable long-term growth.[12]

---

[12] Vandewalle, 2012.

Under Qaddafi, labor laws and financial and business regulations were all largely irrational. The development of non-oil infrastructure had been neglected and the educational system was bloated with students seeking degrees that had little to do with labor-market demand. As in many oil-producing states, subsidies introduced major distortions—especially when it came to gasoline, which at 12 cents per liter on average between 2008 and 2012 was among the cheapest in the world.[13] As a consequence of these policies, Libya's economy is highly distorted and the non-oil sector has remained small. Because few Libyans have been willing to work for lower wages outside the government, official rates of unemployment have been high. In 2010, the official unemployment rate was 13.5 percent, with the percentage of unemployed youth estimated to be twice this number.[14]

Libya needs to pursue regulatory and financial reforms, the establishment of reliable judiciary and property protection legislation, and other measures. Wholesaling, retailing, and oil services present promising opportunities for economic diversification. Tourism is another area in which the Libyan economy might diversify beyond the oil industry, although there are drawbacks.[15] Tourism is the single biggest sector in several neighboring countries, including Tunisia, Morocco, and Egypt. Libya has a beautiful coastline, Roman ruins, and is close to Europe. There are, however, a number of specific obstacles to the development of a tourist industry in Libya, including insecurity; the fact that many of the jobs created by the tourism industry are low-wage; the conservative nature of Libya's society, which prohibits the sale of alcohol; and the fact that European customs, such as beachwear, could offend many Libyans' sense of propriety. Salafists in Libya could easily protest non-segregated beaches, for example, scaring prospective European tourists away.

Like the Gulf States, Libya has used its oil wealth to invest in infrastructure. But the environment for economic growth would be

---

[13] World Bank Development Indicators, data files on the pump price of gasoline in US$ per liter, 2013.

[14] Khan and Mezran, 2013.

[15] For example, see Chami et al., 2012.

improved if the country invested in upgrading its airports and sea-ports, especially if the country opened up opportunities for the private sector to become engaged in investing in and managing these operations. Opening the telecommunications sector and improving the environment for building housing would stimulate economic growth and improve the housing stock.

Most of the jobs for Libyans that would be generated by increased investments in infrastructure would be on the services side: finance, telecommunications, architecture and design, etc. However, despite arguments to the contrary, investment in infrastructure projects would be unlikely to generate jobs for Libyans in construction.[16] Libya has a long, porous border with two of the poorest countries in the world: Chad and Niger. Wages in Egypt and Sudan are also far below those in Libya. Consequently, any jobs in the construction sector generated by an increase in investment will almost certainly go to poorer Arabs or Africans from neighboring countries, not Libyans; unemployed Libyans are unlikely to be willing to take such jobs.

The postwar government has taken some steps toward reform, including relaxing some restrictions on currency convertibility and opening some opportunities for the private sector. However, under pressure from the street, Libyan authorities also increased subsidies for food, fuel, and electricity to 11 percent of GDP. The 2013 budget went even further, raising them to 14 percent of GDP.[17] Government wages have also increased, making employment in the private sector even less appealing. Such measures may be a necessary means of temporarily reducing the chances of conflict while insecurity prevails, but they do so at a risk to Libya's long-term economic health. Meanwhile, the question of the future legal framework for financial industry—and the extent to which *shari'a* in particular will be adopted—remains another unknown that has kept investors at bay. In January 2013, the GNC passed a law—supported by 106 of the 110 delegates present—that forbids interest on all transactions involving state institutions and

---

[16]   Khan and Mezran, 2013.

[17]   Khan and Mezran, 2013.

corporate entities (but *not* individuals).[18] The spokesman for the GNC described this as a first step toward establishing an Islamic banking system.

Provided it does not collapse into another all-out civil war, Libyans will enjoy a fairly high level of income for a post-conflict state on account of its energy resources. Reforming the economy to provide the basis for a more stable polity in which citizens are productively employed in the economy will be more of a challenge.

Moving forward with economic reforms will be difficult, however, until the security situation is brought under control and the political system gains in legitimacy. In the meantime, the best that can be hoped for is that Libya's leadership continues to take steps to liberalize the economy while refraining from further extending subsidies or increasing the government wage bill.

---

[18] "Lībīya Tahzhur al-Fawā'id al-Masrafīya [Libya Prohibits Bank Interest]," *Al-jazeera.net*, January 7, 2013.

CHAPTER FIVE

Alternative Strategies

Libya has not returned to war, but more than two years after Qaddafi's death and on the third anniversary of the outbreak of the revolution, serious insecurity persists, the political process is stalled, and the economic outlook is deteriorating. Libya is clearly in better shape than Syria and some other countries in the region. It is also currently somewhat better off than Iraq, although this is largely due to Iraq's recent deterioration: As Figure 5.1 shows, violence in Libya was higher on a per capita basis at certain points in 2012 than it was in Iraq, although Iraq reclaimed the lead as tensions there escalated in 2013. Within Libya, reported fatalities and conflict incidents have not declined and in fact have risen to levels that, at times, are more than twice those reported in 2012.

The extent to which insecurity has not only become self-perpetuating, but has undermined political-economic stabilization, cannot be understated. Insecurity undermined the legitimacy and effectiveness of both the NTC and the GNC. Because the government was unable even to control the streets of Tripoli, it was constantly subject to the whims of whatever armed group was willing to brandish weapons and threaten officials. The problem extended to the very halls of government itself, where former revolutionaries were able to eavesdrop menacingly on the conversations of parliamentarians. Because the GNC has no security forces of its own, the *thuwwar* were able to occupy the parliament regularly and impose their will on elected officials through intimidation and violence—most notably in the case of the political isolation law, but also in other matters. For example, in April 2012,

Figure 5.1
Violence in Iraq Outstripped Libya in 2013

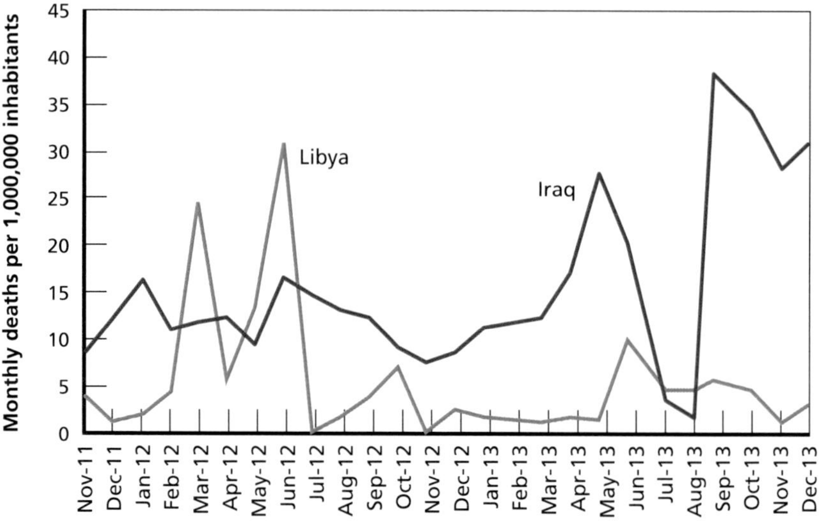

SOURCE: IHS Jane's, "Terrorism and Insurgency Intelligence Centre, JTIC Events
Database," data files on monthly deaths in Libya and Iraq, 2013.
RAND RR577-5.1

militia members attacked the prime minister's headquarters after the
Ministry of Finance moved to limit the number of militia members on
the state payroll.[1] In a similar incident in March 2013, militia members overran the Justice Ministry after the minister suggested that the
state would be taking over prisons operated by *thuwwar.*[2] Government offices and ministers themselves have been the targets of personal
abuse, bomb attacks, and assassinations.

Beyond its direct impact on governance, insecurity also burdened
the government with challenges that were largely beyond its capaci-
ties, creating a major distraction for a government that was already rife
with tension. Responding to the attack on the U.S. diplomatic facil-

---

[1] "Hujūm ala Maqarr Ri'āsat al-Wuzarā' bi Sabab Tawaqquf Minhat al-Thuwār [An Attack
on the Prime Minister's Headquarters Because of Suspension in Compensation to the Revo-
lutionaries]," *Al-Watan al-Libīya*, April 10, 2012.

[2] Mohamed Eljarh, "Libya's Fight for the Rule of Law," *Foreign Policy*, April 4, 2013.

ity in Benghazi consumed a huge amount of the newly elected government's bandwidth. Throughout the first two years after Qaddafi's death, flare-ups of violence repeatedly challenged both the capabilities and the underlying legitimacy and confidence in the new Libyan state. Just as it has undermined the political process, so has insecurity taken a toll on the economy. Not only does it scare foreign investors off, it has threatened oil production and could eventually undermine the solvency of the state, which has been one of the main things Libya has going for it as a postconflict country. Finally, the lack of security, especially after Benghazi, has severely reduced the ability of foreign officials to interface with their Libyan counterparts and has turned Libya into one of the most dangerous posts for U.S. Foreign Service officers, on par with Yemen and other crisis countries.

On one hand, the historical record indicates that the longer Libya goes without a relapse into civil war, the greater its chances of avoiding a relapse altogether.[3] The positive effect created by the passage of time is even stronger in cases where rebels win the war, as they did in Libya.[4] On the other hand, the longer insecurity prevails, the more time potentially violent regional, tribal, and jihadist groups have to gain traction and undermine stabilization. The risks of violent fracture along regional lines, further factionalization, or destabilization by Islamist militants are all still high.

Could an Interim Stabilization Force Have Made a Difference?

Given the severe negative impact that insecurity has had on Libya's postconflict reconstruction, it is worth considering whether a different

---

[3] J. Michael Quinn, T. David Mason, and Mehmet Gurses, "Sustaining the Peace: Determinants of Civil War Recurrence," *International Interactions*, Vol. 33, No. 2, 2007, pp. 167–193; Paul Collier, Anke Hoeffler, and Måns Söderbom, "Post-Conflict Risks," *Journal of Peace Research*, Vol. 45, No.4, 2008, pp. 461–478.

[4] T. David Mason, Mehmet Gurses, Patrick T. Brandt, and Jason Michael Quinn, "When Civil Wars Recur: Conditions for Durable Peace after Civil Wars," *International Studies Perspectives*, Vol. 12, 2011, pp. 171–189.

post-conflict strategy, in particular one involving the deployment of an interim security force immediately after the war, might have yielded better results. A significant body of research has found a correlation between post-conflict success and deployments of peacekeeping forces. To be sure, the relationship between troop deployments and peace is very complex. International peacekeeping and stabilization forces incur political and as well as financial costs and can become a target for spoilers seeking to undermine the peace. But the cost of such deployments needs to be weighed against their positive effects. Not all post-conflict situations are the same, and while troop deployments cannot alone guarantee success, there is good evidence that postwar stabilization forces, especially in the early years following the end of a war, do tend to promote peace.[5]

Such forces can play a variety of different roles, including fighting insurgents, separating warring factions, disarming and demobilizing former combatants, training reliable police and military forces, supporting humanitarian operations and elections, and combating crime and keeping basic law and order. The main reason for deploying post-conflict peacekeeping forces in Libya would have been to establish a neutral protector of the post-conflict security that could defend Libya's transitional institutional arrangements and build confidence in the peace itself. Libya was awash in arms after the war, and the possibility that one group might seek to use violence to impose its political will created inherent insecurity and unease. Post-conflict forces would have helped to overcome that unease, increase willingness to cooperate with the transition process, facilitate the disarmament of rebel forces, and protect the government from the riotous street.

---

[5] Michael W. Doyle and Nicholas Sambanis, *Making War and Building Peace*, Princeton, N.J.: Princeton University Press, 2006, pp. 128–129; Collier, Hoeffler and Söderbom, 2008; James Dobbins, Seth G. Jones, Keith Crane, and Beth Cole DeGrasse, *The Beginner's Guide to Nation-Building*, Santa Monica, Calif.: RAND Corporation, MG-557-SRF, 2007; Quinn, Mason, and Gurses, 2007; Caroline Hartzell, Matthew Hoddie, and Donald Rothchild, "Stabilizing the Peace After Civil War: An Investigation of Some Key Variables," *International Organization*, Vol. 55, No. 1, 2001, pp. 183–208; Virginia Page Fortna, "Does Peacekeeping Keep Peace? International Intervention and the Duration of Peace After Civil War," *International Studies Quarterly*, Vol. 48, No. 2, 2004, pp. 269–292; Roland Paris, "Saving Liberal Peacebuilding," *Review of International Studies*, Vol. 36, 2010, pp. 337–365.

How Big a Force Would Have Been Needed?

How big an international force would have been necessary to carry out these tasks? Accurately estimating force requirements for multinational stabilization operations is difficult, and a wide variety of factors can play a role in determining needs. The 2008 U.S. Army Field Manual recommends a ratio of 20 troops per 1,000 inhabitants as a rule of thumb.[6] This is a very crude way of estimating, however, that can both over and understate the necessary size of the force. Many successful post-conflict peacekeeping deployments have been smaller in proportion to the size of the local population, showing that even small international troop deployments can help overcome the kind of insecurity that Libya faced after the war.[7] In cases where local capacity is relatively high, the postwar economic outlook is promising, and the conflict has ended with a negotiated peace accepted by all parties, large numbers of foreign troops may not be necessary.

The UN has had success with stabilization forces at much smaller ratios. For example, in East Timor, the UN deployed a successful stabilization force at a 10:1,000 ratio. A similar ratio in Libya would have meant 61,550 foreign troops. In both Sierra Leone and Namibia, a ratio of 3:1,000 succeeded. A corresponding ratio for Libya would be 18,465. In Cambodia, the ratio was even lower: 2:1,000, yielding a Libyan equivalent of 12,310 total foreign forces. It is worth noting that forces at even lower levels have been successful in Mozambique and El Salvador.

Force requirements vary widely because a multitude of factors affect the situation beyond population size. The 20:1,000 ratio does not, for example, account for the underlying degree of tension of a particular country, the geography of the armed groups, the quality and technological capabilities of the occupying force, or the level of ambi-

---

[6]   U.S. Army, *Field Manual 3.0: Operations*, Washington, D.C.: Headquarters, Department of the Army, February 2008; James T. Quinlivan, "Force Requirements in Stability Operations," *Parameters*, Winter 1995, pp. 59–69.

[7]   Jack Snyder and Robert Jervis, "Civil War and the Security Dilemma," in Barbara F. Walter and Jack Snyder, eds., *Civil Wars, Insecurity, and Intervention*, New York: Columbia University Press, September 2009, pp. 15–37.

tion of the force. More scholarship is needed to understand how these factors work,[8] but there are at least four reasons that a smaller-scale stabilization force might have had a positive impact in Libya.

First, there is reason to believe that intentions of most of the major armed groups after the war were more or less benign. If one believes these groups were so entrenched at the end of the war and forcible disarmament would have been required in the majority of cases, then a large force would clearly have been needed. If, however, most militias—at least at the outset—were unwilling to disarm because they distrusted each other's intentions, feared for their own security, or did not trust the transitional government, then a smaller force could have had a significant impact simply by building trust and alleviating those fears.

At liberation, all indications were that Libya was a case of the latter. As Chapter Two notes, most of the rebel forces that refused to disarm cited their own insecurity, the need to provide security to the population, concerns that pro-Qaddafi forces would return, or general lack of confidence in the chances for the political transition as reasons for not disarming. There was a widespread sense that most of the militias—though not all—did in fact have benign or relatively benign intentions. This is not to claim that there were no differences of opinion about the future direction of the country, only that these differences were not irreconcilable and most groups did not seem intent on imposing their will on the country by force. The jihadist groups that did favor violence as a means for achieving their political objectives were still largely confined to the east, were small in number, and lacked support from even many of the more conservative Islamist groups.

Second, the 20:1,000 rule of thumb is predicated on requirements for fighting a national insurgency in difficult urban conditions. However, when Qaddafi was killed, there was no insurgency in Libya. Instead, the environment was permissive by most historical standards. Because of the large number of arms circulating the country, the situation was less permissive than Germany after World War II, where a ratio of 2:1,000 (13,000 for Libya's population) succeeded. Yet, because

---

[8]   Steven M. Goode, "A Historical Basis for Force Requirements in Counterinsurgency," *Parameters*, Winter 2009–10, pp. 45–57.

Libya's rebels had won an outright victory and had not been fighting each other during the war, the situation was far more permissive than the prevailing situation in Bosnia or Kosovo, two of NATO's more recent interventions where stabilization forces were deployed in significant numbers. Although some differences between the rebel groups had arisen during the war—notably when rebel commander Abdel Fatah Younes was killed in July 2011—the rebels had continued to cooperate in their common effort to overthrow the regime.

Third, although the armed groups themselves were strong in relation to the civilian population and government, they would not have been strong in relation to a moderately well equipped interim security force. As discussed in Chapter Two, rebel fighters were still inexperienced, and the weapons they knew how to use, although plentiful, were mostly small arms. Although the revolutionaries themselves enjoyed high levels of support from the Libyan public, armed groups did not.[9] Most Libyans wanted to see them disarm, as witnessed at intervals over the course of the next two years, when citizens repeatedly protested against entrenched militias.

Fourth, a stabilization force would not necessarily have needed to be deployed nationwide. Even if limited to Tripoli, a force could still have offered many benefits in defusing the tensions that later emerged between armed groups there. In addition to deterring conflict, it could also have provided mediation and confidence-building measures to help alleviate tensions and avoid accidents.[10] Critically, a force that was deployed to the capital alone would have been able to provide security for the government, which, lacking proper guards, was constantly threatened by protests from the street.

Based on this, it is possible to sketch three basic options for what a post-conflict stabilization force might have looked like. Option one is a force that would have deployed to Tripoli alone. Its primary missions would have been:

---

[9] See National Democratic Institute, 2013a; National Democratic Institute, "Seeking Security: Public Opinion Survey in Libya," November 2013b.

[10] See Virginia Page Fortna, *Does Peacekeeping Work? Shaping Belligerents' Choices After Civil War*, Princeton, N.J.: Princeton University Press, 2008, pp.173–179.

1. stabilize the capital, including by deterring conflict between the rebel groups there
2. mediate disputes and support confidence-building measures between the militias
3. provide security at the airport and port
4. secure government buildings from armed protestors
5. conduct crowd control operations when necessary
6. conduct small-scale counterterrorism operations
7. support security sector reform.

A detailed and in-depth assessment of the force requirements for these tasks is beyond the scope of this paper, but some rough estimates are possible for illustrative purposes. Requirements for task 1 would have been the most onerous, likely requiring several thousand troops deployed citywide. (Most could probably have been light infantry, given the rebels' lack of arms, but some medium–heavy armor would also have been desirable for deterrence.) If the Sierra Leone ratio is taken as a model, the force size for these tasks in the capital would need to be 4,557. Because some of the armed groups in Tripoli neared this size, a more substantial force might have been necessary for deterrence, for example, a force sized on the East Timor model of a little more than 15,000. A significant number of these forces would have needed to be gendarmes or formed police units, especially for tasks 4 and 5, as well as task 7. Logistics requirements would have been more challenging than deployments in the Balkans, but nowhere on the level of difficulty required for supplying forces in Afghanistan or sub-Saharan Africa, given Libya's proximity to Europe, many ports, and sound infrastructure. (Because the main jihadist groups were still located far from the capital at that time, task 6 would have required operations outside Tripoli using smaller numbers of high-end, Western forces.)

A second option would have included other major cities on the Mediterranean coastline. The most important city would have been Benghazi, where tensions continued to simmer after the war, for reasons explained below. Two thousand troops might have been sufficient to secure Benghazi (using the Sierra Leone model), but likely a force of a little over 6,000 (the East Timor model) would have been needed due to the underlying tensions between some groups there and the proximity to jihadists in Derna. Force requirements for Misrata and Zintan, two other major power centers, would have been significantly less, both because these are smaller cities and because tensions in them were minimal, if any, after the war. A minimal presence would have been sufficient. Total requirements for this model would therefore be in the environment of 24,000 forces.

A third option, extending deployment of peacekeeping forces to the whole country, would have required not only more forces but significantly more mobility and greater logistical capacity, given the long distances between the urban centers on the Mediterranean coast and the southern provinces. Had international actors attempted such a mission, a force of at least 61,000 (the East Timor ratio) probably would have been needed, and possibly a larger force, especially if an effort was made to assist Libyan authorities in monitoring, let alone controlling, the country's vast and porous borders.

It is reasonable to believe, however, that even the smaller effort, and certainly the medium-sized effort, would have been beneficial in creating space for disarmament, demobilization and reintegration, and security sector reform. Most of all, it would have enabled the government to go about its business without the constant threat of attack from the street.

This is not to argue that deploying a stabilization force would have been easy or risk free. To the contrary, the options sketched above all involve real risks. In general, the risks are greater the smaller the stabilization force, although there is no straightforward inverse relationship between troop levels and risks, since larger troop deployments more easily become targets for spoilers, even if they provide broader and more effective territorial coverage. The main risk of the first option would have been that violence outside Tripoli may have forced international coalition leaders to choose between expanding the force and being accused of "creeping intervention," withdrawing the force and appearing to accept defeat, or staying the course and being accused of impotence or hypocrisy. The second option would provide some guarantees against this, but at a higher cost. The third option would provide the greatest guarantees, although at the highest cost by far. It would also have been the most difficult to sell to the Libyan people and the most liable to draw insurgent attacks.

Risks obviously need to be weighed against benefits, which could have been significant. An effective interim security force would have saved Libya's nascent democratic institutions from constant humiliation and interference from the street and increased confidence in their durability and level of support from the international community. It would also have facilitated rebel disarmament by ensuring the security of those who disarmed. An interim security force could also have gotten started on dealing with the problem of jihadist groups in the east. In general, it would have helped to alleviate fear and mistrust and might have improved confidence "merely by existing" if the deployment was seen as a symbol of a shared commitment to peace among the armed groups, not to mention the international community.[11] If deployed early enough, it could also have undertaken the critical mission of securing some of Qaddafi's weapon stockpiles and thus reduced the number of arms circulating around the country.

Not least of all, if such a force succeeded in enhancing security, it would have made a much larger foreign civilian presence possible. This, in turn, would have afforded greater opportunity to transfer key knowledge about public administration, political process, security sector reform, and other areas to the new Libyan officials. The international community would have had more leverage to shape the political process, encourage strong public demand for progress, and help steer the nation toward stability. In the absence of such leverage, the international impact on Libya's post-conflict path has been extremely limited.

Would Such a Force Have Been Feasible?

The question of what the size and missions of a postwar stabilization force in Libya would have been should be considered separately from whether such a force would have been politically feasible to generate in

---

[11] For a discussion of how peacekeeping helps "merely by existing," see Fortna, *Does Peacekeeping Work*, p.177.

the fall of 2011. The problems of generating forces and finding funding arise in all such situations, but amidst a financial crisis in Europe and given ongoing operations in Afghanistan, the challenge was especially large for Western leaders at the time the issue arose.

Given the aforementioned considerations, there is no reason a force would have had to be composed exclusively, or even primarily, of troops from NATO countries. Indeed, a UN force would have been preferable, and it would have been preferable for the majority of the troops to be supplied by regional powers or Muslim states, such as Jordan or perhaps Malaysia. Officers from NATO member nations might have provided guidance on security sector reform and taken responsibility for counterterrorism operations, but the quantitative force requirements for these tasks would have been much lower than for others. If a UN force was not possible, a force under a lead nation would have been a good alternative. Turkey might have played a particularly constructive role here.

To carry out the tasks above, the force would also have needed an appropriate Chapter VII UN Security Council mandate. This would have required at least tacit Russian and Chinese support. This might have been difficult, given their carping about the NATO operation during the war, but exactly how difficult is hard to say, because no such effort was ever made.[12]

The biggest obstacle to a post-conflict deployment of peacekeeping forces in Libya, however, was arguably the reticence of the Libyan government to invite such a force, a problem that seriously compounded the others. Libyan authorities wrongly, though not surprisingly, feared that their country might end up "occupied" in the way that Iraq had been. The NTC worried that its legitimacy might be further eroded by the presence of an outside force. There were also legitimate concerns that a stabilization force could become a target for extremists and other spoilers seeking to undermine stabilization.

These are serious concerns, and it would have been unwise to deploy a stabilization force without some invitation from the Libyan government. Nevertheless, the Libyan government was in a very weak

---

[12] Interviews with U.S. officials, February 2012.

position to say no to NATO states, especially when Qaddafi was still at large and NATO air operations were still underway. Had Western governments themselves been more committed to deploying such a force, it is very difficult to imagine that they would not have been able to arrange an invitation from the Libyan government under these conditions, especially for a more limited force. It is also unclear how broadly the reticence about an interim security force was shared within the NTC. There is some indication that not all members of the NTC thought it was wise to reject the idea outright.[13] In practice, however, the Libyan reticence about post-conflict peacekeepers stopped international discussion of the issue and there appears to have been no effort to convince the Libyan authorities that their interests would be better served by some form of stabilization force.[14] A key lesson for the future is to begin discussions about post-conflict security deployments early on, while international leverage is still greatest. This will not be easy, but it needs to be tried.

Conclusion

There are a number of sound arguments for taking a limited approach to post-conflict stabilization.[15] Post-conflict stabilization deployments are costly, infringe on national sovereignty, can generate resentment, and inevitably create problems of their own. Advocates of a strictly limited international role argue, for example, that smaller-scale interventions are more likely to succeed because their lower cost will allow them to be sustained over a longer period of time. They also point to the economic distortions that outsized international civilian and military missions can introduce into a fragile post-conflict economy.

---

[13] Interview with former staff member of the NTC, November 27, 2013.

[14] Interview with former western official, November 18, 2013.

[15] For a summary of some of these arguments, see Stephen Watts, Caroline Baxter, Molly Dunigan, and Christopher Rizzi, *The Uses and Limits of Small-Scale Military Interventions*, Santa Monica, Calif.: RAND Corporation, MG-1226-RC, 2012, pp. 15–25.

The most common argument, however, is that large foreign military deployments inevitably engender a nationalist backlash.[16]

The very light international footprint in Libya, however, has not worked well. International actors may have spared themselves short-term pain and cost, but that savings comes at the risk of longer-term regional instability and the strategic interests of all those countries that participated in the initial NATO intervention. In retrospect, it is difficult to see how a peaceful process of institutional development on the scale that was required in Libya could take place in the absence of basic security. At the same time, it is difficult to imagine how security can be provided after a war in a country that lacks basic political and security institutions, without at least some direct international military support.

Strategists and military planners should have no illusions about this as they look ahead. To avoid incurring unsustainable costs, and still meet the demand for intervention and statebuilding activities, the United States and its allies will need to continue investing in the development of effective interim security forces in postwar situations—not only their own, but also through other organizations like the United Nations. They may also need to grow more accustomed to the risks that lower-cost operations will likely entail.

---

[16] Nora Bensahel, "Preventing Insurgencies After Major Combat," *Defence Studies*, Vol. 6, No. 3, 2006; Rory Stewart and Gerald Knaus, *Can Intervention Work?* New York: Norton, 2011; David Kilcullen, *The Accidental Guerilla*, New York: Oxford University Press, 2009.

CHAPTER SIX

Libya's Future Path—Steps for the International Community

The United States and its allies have both moral and strategic interests in ensuring that Libya does not collapse back into violence or become a haven for jihadist groups within striking distance of Europe. Increased terrorist violence in Libya would have a terrible impact on the already fragile Sahel region, which has become increasingly susceptible to jihadist activities in the last decade. A standoff between major militia-backed groups that plunges the country back into civil war would have similarly negative consequences, as would the emergence of another autocratic ruler of the Qaddafi mold. Needless to say, if Libya—or the broader region, for that matter—were to become a haven for terrorists, it would be a serious problem for the West.

In contrast, gradual political stabilization under representative government and constitutional rule would allow continued benefit from Libya's energy and other resources, while greatly strengthening the region as a whole. Despite its current challenges, Libya still has many advantages when compared with other post-conflict societies that increase the chances that the situation there could improve. For example, it can still foot the bill for much of its post-conflict needs—even if it currently lacks the administrative capacity to manage complex payments to foreign entities. Its relatively small population is also a reason for optimism, as is its proximity to Europe. Many Libyans remain, moreover, generally pro-American in their outlook, general distrust of foreign influence notwithstanding.

Although Libya's future is ultimately up to the Libyans them-selves, the United States and its allies can do certain things to improve the chances of a positive outcome.

Provide Support for a National Reconciliation Process

It is imperative that the elected Libyan government and its interna-tional partners redouble their efforts to get control over Libya's security situation. Disarmament, demobilization, and reintegration is still sorely needed, but repeating empty declarations that it must happen will not work. Far-reaching security sector reform is also needed, but neither are likely to happen in the absence of some semblance of security.

Security could be strengthened in Libya by outside actors, but the costs would likely now exceed those outlined in the previous chapter, which have so far proven too much for the international community to muster. Security could also emerge from the dominance of one armed group over the others, but this would come only after a return to civil war and thus be a cure as bad as the disease.

Alternatively, groups in Libya could come to a political agreement that alleviates tensions and includes concrete steps to improve security. At present, this seems the best and most reasonable option, even if challenging itself.

Libya's leaders and their international backers should thus con-sider using a national reconciliation process that would complement the constitution-making process; help build trust between various tribal, regional, and other social forces and armed groups; and thereby facilitate disarmament. International actors would also benefit from the information gleaned regarding the militias and their aims.

Such a process could help engage civil society in constitution-making discussions. It could also be used as a vehicle for building trust between armed groups and the tribal and other social forces aligned with them. Although the process would have to be driven largely by the Libyans themselves, outside actors, such as the UN or EU, would need to play a critical facilitating or mediating role.

To encourage participation, some of the issues on the table should involve decisions about access to power within the new Libyan state—for example, discussions of the future of Libya's heretofore underdeveloped and indeterminate security structures. Although this might require revisiting some of the discussions regarding the structure of the security system within Libya, opening these discussions to a wider range of actors might be a helpful way of encouraging broad participation. Objectives of such a process could include:

- Provide a vehicle for the broader Libyan public to demand further rebel disarmament, stronger political institutions, and improvements in the country's public administration.
- Reduce the number of arms circulating in the country. Although a conference would be very unlikely to eliminate all the arms in the country, it might at least help to reduce the number of arms in major population centers.
- Establish rules of the road and obtain guarantees against the use of violence in political deliberations. Such guarantees would provide critical space for the national deliberations over the constitution. Absent such guarantees, this process is vulnerable to the same kind of interference that led to the political isolation law.
- Build trust and increase information exchange between different armed groups regarding their capabilities and intentions. This would likely help to reduce overall tensions.

Ideally, the process would be led by a high-level European diplomat, such as Paddy Ashdown, or another figure of international stature from the Muslim world. The success of such a process would not be guaranteed and would depend on several factors, including international support, timing, finding the right person to lead it, and chance. Nevertheless, among the options on the table, it is one of the best.

Strengthen Libya's National Security Forces

Because Libya's security forces are weak and have no way to train themselves, in the late winter of 2013 Prime Minister Zeidan made a formal request to several countries for military training. At the June 2013 G8 summit, a number of countries agreed to provide training for Libyan military and police, paid for by the Libyan government. The United States will provide basic training for 5,000–8,000 Libyan soldiers in Bulgaria, while the UK announced it will train an initial 2,000, with more to follow.[1] Italy will train 2,000 and Turkey 3,000. Training in both these countries has already started. Training this "general-purpose force" will yield a force of approximately 15,000 over the next several years.

Providing this training is essential to building a stronger Libyan state. Some analysts in the United States nevertheless expressed reservations about the wisdom of helping the Libyans train their forces, both on the grounds that the forces might not meet U.S. human rights standards, and the possibility that they would simply become "another militia."[2] It is true that stronger government forces might be seen as a threat to some militias. There will also always be a risk that some troops might not behave according to western standards at some point down the line—if so, it would not be a first.

If pursued carefully and alongside a political process, however, the benefits of such training will outweigh the possible costs. Libya simply cannot have an effective state without competent security forces. The effort deserves the full support of the United States and its NATO allies. At the time of writing, however, these efforts are either not funded or underfunded and the Libyans—who have promised to pay for a large part of the training—have found it difficult to fulfill their own end of the bargain.

Increasing the throughput for this program will be desirable, but will be constrained by the ability of the Libyan government to vet and

---

[1] Interview with U.S. official, Washington, D.C., December 17, 2013.

[2] Frederic Wehrey and Peter Cole, *Building Libya's Security Sector*, Washington, D.C.: Carnegie Endowment for International Peace, August 2013.

identify candidates for the training programs. Because the administrative capacity of the Libyan state is so low, and the government's grip on power so weak, spoilers at almost any level can slow down the process. Police training will also take place, with the UK intending to train large numbers of investigative police.[3] NATO Secretary General Anders Fogh Rasmussen met with Zeidan in September 2013 and discussed the possibility of further NATO participation in these efforts. Reports that the United States was already training an elite counter-terrorism force in limited numbers resurfaced in September 2013, when media outlets reported that military equipment had been stolen from a base where U.S. special operations forces were training Libyan personnel.[4] If true, such efforts are also worthwhile, provided the trainees are properly vetted, supported, and eventually embedded within a sound institutional framework.

International effort cannot, however, be limited to training overseas alone. It will also be necessary to help the Libyan government lay the groundwork for the deployment of these forces within Libya itself in order to minimize potential frictions with armed groups.

The process of training reliable security forces will take a long time. The adequacy of potential recruits will no doubt be an issue—especially if the tribulations that befell efforts to train Libyan police in Jordan are any indicator. It will remain important to ensure that the process of vetting recruits produces a balanced representation of the major parties on the ground, lest one side begin to perceive the effort as being directed against it.

---

3 Interview with UK official, via telephone, September 6, 2013.

4 Ashraf Abdul Wahab and Nigel Ash, "Weaponry Plundering Prompts U.S. Training Withdrawal," *Libya Herald*, September 17, 2013; "Sensitive Weapons Stolen from US Special Forces in Libya May Have Fallen in Wrong Hands," *Tripolipost.com*, September 15, 2013. See also Eric Schmitt, "U.S. to Help Create an Elite Libyan Force to Combat Islamic Extremists," *The New York Times*, October 15, 2012.

Help Libya Strengthen Border Security

Border security also remains a major, related challenge. The porousness of Libya's borders and their susceptibility to smuggling and the circulation of criminals and jihadists will continue to undermine Libyan and regional security. Improvements will take time and require building institutional capacity within the Libyan state as well as investments in monitoring capabilities, such as intelligence, surveillance, and reconnaissance platforms. The establishment of an effective, modern border-management system, with all its legal and administrative requirements, will be far more difficult given the sorry state of Libya's legal and administrative structures.

The EU Border Assistance Mission (EUBAM) is equipped for training and assisting the Libyan government in Tripoli, but has neither been staffed to its fully approved level nor been able to interface effectively with the Libyan government. The EU intended to deploy 110 personnel to this end but as yet has put only 45 staff in place, and these were confined to the Corinthia Hotel in Tripoli and had limited contact with their Libyan counterparts.[5] At the time of writing the majority of these were temporarily removed from the country due to security concerns.[6] This does not bode well for the mission's ability to strengthen borders thousands of kilometers from Tripoli.

Borders are nevertheless an area where foreign knowledge and capability can be beneficial. The EU has a special interest in helping Libya on this issue, given its geographic proximity—a fact the drowning of hundreds of sub-Saharan migrants from Libya off the coast of Italy in October 2013 again reminded the world.

---

[5]   "EU Border Assistance Mission Falters," *Maghreb Confidential*, October 24, 2013; Gaub, 2013.

[6]   Interview with EU official, Paris, January 17, 2014.

Help Libya Strengthen Its Public Administration

International actors are also well positioned to help Libya improve its public administration. UN Special Representative to Libya Tarek Mitri has rightly identified this type of institution building as an area in which the Libyan government could stand to make significant gains from international assistance.[7]

In addition to having an abiding interest in Libya, the EU and its member states are in a good position for this particular type of work, due to their proximity to Libya, which makes it easier to deploy civilian staff. The EU and its member states could significantly increase their level of effort—although doing so will likely have to await an improvement in the security situation. In addition to building institutions at the national level, an effort should also be made to work with and strengthen institutions at the local level, which in some cases are more functional than those in Tripoli.

Prepare for the Possibility of Another Intervention

Sadly, the possibility that Libya could descend again into civil war is not that remote. The country is not there now, and war can still be averted with the right approach and some good fortune. Nevertheless, if major militias come to loggerheads, or jihadists further their grip on certain areas, violence could escalate. International actors should be prepared to again take steps to contain widespread violence and protect the Libyan people from the humanitarian crisis that would result. Preferably, this responsibility would fall to the United Nations, but if discord on the Security Council prevents the deployment of a full peacekeeping mission with the requisite mandate, then NATO and the European Union will need to act independently, preferably in conjunction with the Gulf Cooperation Council and Arab League—as in the initial operation that toppled Qaddafi.

---

[7] Interview with Tarek Mitri, Tripoli, February 3, 2013.

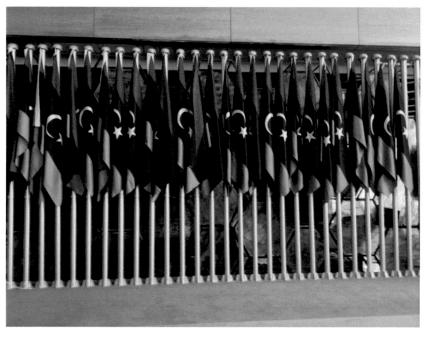

Libyan flags displayed in the GNC (Photo by Christopher Chivvis).

RAND *RR577-6.1*

Bibliography

African Economic Outlook, *Balance of Payments Indicators, 2010–2013,* June 6, 2013. As of October 10, 2013:
http://www.africaneconomicoutlook.org/en/data-statistics/table-6-balance-of-payments-indicators-2010-2013/

Ahmed, Akbar, and Frankie Martin, "Understanding the Sanusi of Cyrenaica," Al Jazeera.com, March 26, 2012.

Al-Khalidi, Suleiman, and Julia Payne, "Update 2-Libya Struggles to Resume Oil Exports," Reuters, September 16, 2013.

Al-Manara, "Istitlāʿ lil Rāʾī Yuzhir Anna Akthar min 64% min Istatalaʿat Arāʿihim maʿ Qānūn al-ʿAzl al-Siyāsī fī Lībīya [An Opinion Poll Shows That More Than 64% of Those Polled Are for the Political Isolation Law in Libya]," March 7, 2013.

Al Qaeda in Libya: A Profile, Federal Research Division, Library of Congress, August 2012.

Al-Shaheibi, Rami, "Eastern Libya Pulls Away from Central Government," Associated Press, March 6, 2012.

Ashour, Omar, "Libyan Islamists Unpacked," *Brookings Doha Center Policy Briefing,* May 2012.

"Bani Walid Fighters Stage Sit-in, Call for Libyan Defence Minister's Dismissal," *BBC Monitoring Middle East,* January 28, 2012.

Bass, Gary J., *Freedom's Battle: The Origins of Humanitarian Intervention,* New York: Knopf, 2008.

Bates, Robert H., *When Things Fell Apart: State Failure in Late-Century Africa,* Cambridge, UK: Cambridge University Press, 2008.

Bensahel, Nora, "Preventing Insurgencies After Major Combat," *Defence Studies,* Vol. 6, No. 3, 2006.

Benotman, Noman, Jason Pack, and James Brandon, "Islamists" in Jason Pack, ed., *The 2011 Libyan Uprisings and the Struggle for the Post-Qadhafi Future,* New York: Palgrave, 2013.

Black, Ian, Chris McGreal, and Harriet Sherwood, "Libyan Rebels Supplied with Anti-Tank Weapons by Qatar," *The Guardian*, April 14, 2011.

Bremner, Charles, and Wil Crisp, "Chaos Turns Libya into Back Door for Migrants," *The Times*, October 17, 2013, p. 37.

Central Intelligence Agency, "Africa: Libya," *The World Factbook*, 2013. As of September 20, 2013:
https://www.cia.gov/library/publications/the-world-factbook/geos/ly.html

Chami, Ralph, Ahmed Al-Darwish, Serhan Cevik, Joshua Charap, Susan George, Borja Gracia, Simon Gray, and Sailendra Pattanayak, *Libya Beyond the Revolution: Challenges and Opportunities*, Washington, D.C.: International Monetary Fund, 2012. As of September 20, 2013:
http://www.imf.org/external/pubs/ft/dp/2012/1201mcd.pdf

Champeaux, Nicolas, "Le Sud de la Libye, Nouveau Sanctuaire des Jihadistes," *RFI*, February 5, 2014.

Chivvis, Christopher S., "A Year After the Fall of Tripoli, Libya Still Fragile," CNN.com, August 23, 2012. As of October 18, 2013:
http://globalpublicsquare.blogs.cnn.com/2012/08/23/a-year-after-the-fall-of-tripoli-libya-still-fragile/

———, *Toppling Qaddafi: Libya and the Limits of Liberal Intervention*, New York: Cambridge University Press, 2014.

Chivvis, Christopher S., and Andrew Liepman, *North Africa's Menace: AQIM's Evolution and the U.S. Policy Response*, Santa Monica, Calif.: RAND Corporation, RR-415-OSD, 2013. As of October 18, 2013:
http://www.rand.org/pubs/research_reports/RR415.html

Chivvis, Christopher S., Keith Crane, Peter Mandaville, and Jeffrey Martini, *Libya's Post Qaddafi Transition: The Nation-Building Challenge*, Santa Monica, Calif.: RAND Corporation, RR-129-SRF, November 2012. As of September 23, 2013:
http://www.rand.org/pubs/research_reports/RR129.html

Chorin, Ethan, *Exit the Colonel: The Hidden History of the Libyan Revolution*, New York: Public Affairs, 2012.

Coker, Margaret, "Militant Suspected in Attack in Libya Remains at Large," *Wall Street Journal*, October 17, 2012, p. A1.

Collier, Paul, Anke Hoeffler, and Måns Söderbom, "Post-Conflict Risks," *Journal of Peace Research*, Vol. 45, No. 4, 2008, pp. 461–478.

Coughlin, Con, "Al Qaeda in the Age of Obama," *Wall Street Journal*, December 7, 2012.

Cristiani, Dario, *The Zintan Militia and the Fragmented Libyan State*, Washington, D.C.: Jamestown Foundation, January 19, 2012. As of October 18, 2013: http://www.jamestown.org/uploads/media/Zintan_Brigade_Grey.pdf

Daalder, Ivo H., and James G. Stavridis, "NATO's Victory in Libya," *Foreign Affairs*, March/April 2012.

Dagher, Sam, Charles Levinson, and Margaret Coker, "Tiny Kingdom's Huge Role in Libya Draws Concern," *Wall Street Journal*, October 17, 2011.

Denyer, Simon, "Libyan Militias Amass Weapons from Unsecured Depots," *Washington Post*, September 22, 2011, p. A11.

Dobbins, James, Seth G. Jones, Keith Crane, and Beth Cole DeGrasse, *The Beginner's Guide to Nation-Building*, Santa Monica, Calif.: RAND Corporation, MG-557-SRF, 2007. As of October 18, 2013: http://www.rand.org/pubs/monographs/MG557.html

Doherty, Megan, "Building a New Libya: Citizen Views on Libya's Electoral and Political Process," National Democratic Institute, May 2012a.

———, "Give Us Change We Can See: Citizen Views on Libya's Political Process," National Democratic Institute, December 2012b;

Donais, Timothy, "Empowerment or Imposition? Dilemmas of Local Ownership in Post-Conflict Peacebuilding Processes," *Peace and Change*, Vol. 34, No. 1, January 2009.

Doyle, Michael W., and Nicholas Sambanis, *Making War and Building Peace*, Princeton, N.J.: Princeton University Press, 2006. As of October 18, 2013: http://press.princeton.edu/titles/8196.html

Draft Constitutional Charter for the Transitional Stage [Libya], September 2011. As of August 8, 2013: http://www.refworld.org/docid/4e80475b2.html

Duffey, Tamara, "Cultural Issues in Contemporary Peacekeeping," *International Peacekeeping*, Vol. 7, No. 1, 2000.

"Eastern Libya Pulls Away from Central Govt," *New Zealand Herald*, March 7, 2012.

Eljarh, Mohamed, "Libya's Fight for the Rule of Law," *Foreign Policy*, April 4, 2013. As of January 22, 2014: http://transitions.foreignpolicy.com/posts/2013/04/04/libya_s_fight_for_the_rule_of_law

Engel, Andrew, "A Way Forward in Benghazi," Washington Institute for Near East Policy, *PolicyWatch* 2088, June 12, 2013. As of January 20, 2014: http://www.washingtoninstitute.org/policy-analysis/view/a-way-forward-in-benghazi

Englebert, Pierre, and Denis M. Tull, "Postconflict Reconstruction in Africa: Flawed Ideas About Failed States," *International Security*, Vol. 32, No. 4, 2008.

Essul, Seraj, "Oil Exports Down to 160,000 Barrels per Day: Oil Ministry," *Libya Herald*, September 1, 2013. As of September 20, 2013: http://www.libyaherald.com/2013/09/01/ oil-exports-down-to-160000-barrels-per-day-oil-ministry/#axzz2fSvIH7HH

"EU Border Assistance Mission Falters," *Maghreb Confidential*, October 24, 2013.

Evans-Pritchard, E. E., *The Sanusi of Cyrenaica*, Oxford, UK: Oxford University Press, 1954.

Fahim, Kareem, "Libyan Town Under Siege Is a Center of Resistance to the New Government," *The New York Times*, October 21, 2012a. As of October 18, 2013: http://www.nytimes.com/2012/10/22/world/africa/libyan-town-under-siege-is-a-center-of-resistance.html

———, "Libyan Forces Now Control Restive Town, Officials Say," *The New York Times*, October 24, 2012b. As of October 18, 2013: http://www.nytimes.com/2012/10/25/world/africa/libyan-forces-now-control-bani-walid-officials-say.html

Fearon, James D., and David D. Laitin, "Ethnicity, Insurgency, and Civil War," *American Political Science Review*, Vol. 97, No. 1, February 2003.

Flores, Thomas Edward, and Ifran Nooruddin, "The Effect of Elections on Postconflict Peace and Reconstruction," *The Journal of Politics*, Vol. 74, No. 2, April 2012.

Fornaji, Hadi, "Blockades Polarizing Libya; Militiamen Now Hit Electricity Ministry," *Libya Herald*, May 2, 2013.

Fortna, Virginia Page, "Does Peacekeeping Keep Peace? International Intervention and the Duration of Peace After Civil War," *International Studies Quarterly*, Vol. 48, No. 2, 2004, pp. 269–292.

———, *Does Peacekeeping Work? Shaping Belligerents' Choices After Civil War*, Princeton, N.J.: Princeton University Press, 2008, pp. 173–179.

Frykberg, Mel, "Libya's Vow to Reign in Militias Is Immediately Challenged," *Christian Science Monitor*, September 24, 2012.

Fukuyama, Francis, *America at the Crossroads: Democracy, Power, and the Neoconservative Legacy*, New Haven, Conn.: Yale University Press, 2006.

Gaub, Florence, "Libya: The Struggle for Security," *EUISS Brief*, June 2013.

General National Congress, "Al-Mu'tamar al-Watanī al-ʿĀmm Yuqirr Qānūn al-ʿAzl al-Siyāsī [The GNC Approves the Political Isolation Law]," May 5, 2013. As of February 6, 2014: http://www.gnc.gov.ly/legislation_files/635131800553722968.pdf

GNC—*See* General National Congress.

Goode, Steven M., "A Historical Basis for Force Requirements in Counterinsurgency," *Parameters*, Winter 2009–10, pp. 45–57.

Goodspeed, Peter, "Libyan Weapons May Soon Be in Terrorist Hands," *National Post*, September 9, 2011, p. A1.

"Guide to Libya's Militias," *BBC Online*, September 28, 2012.

Hartzell, Caroline, Matthew Hoddie, and Donald Rothchild, "Stabilizing the Peace After Civil War: An Investigation of Some Key Variables," *International Organization*, Vol. 55, No. 1, 2001.

Hookham, Mark, "MI6 Warns Libyan Arms Dumps Are 'Tesco for World Terrorists,'" *The Sunday Times*, June 16, 2013.

"Hujūm ala Maqarr Ri'āsat al-Wuzarā' bi Sabab Tawaqquf Minhat al-Thuwār [An Attack on the Prime Minister's Headquarters Because of Suspension in Compensation to the Revolutionaries]," *Al-Watan al-Libīya*, April 10, 2012.

Humphreys, Macartan, Jeffrey D. Sachs, and Joseph E. Stiglitz, *Escaping the Resource Curse*, New York: Columbia University Press, 2007.

IHS Jane's, "Terrorism and Insurgency Intelligence Centre, JTIC Events Database," data files on monthly deaths in Libya and Iraq, 2013.

International Crisis Group, "Holding Libya Together: Security Challenges After Qadhafi," Crisis Group Middle East/North Africa Report No. 115, December 14, 2011. As of October 10, 2013:
http://www.crisisgroup.org/~/media/Files/Middle%20East%20North%20Africa/North%20Africa/115%20Holding%20Libya%20Together%20--%20Security%20Challenges%20after%20Qadhafi.pdf

———, "Divided We Stand," Middle East/North Africa Report No. 130, September 14, 2012.

International Organization for Migration, "IOM Response to the Libyan Crisis," *External Situation Report*, October 31, 2011.

International Stabilisation Response Team, Department for International Development (UK), "Libya: 20 May–30 June 2011," 2011. As of October 9, 2013:
https://www.gov.uk/government/uploads/system/uploads/attachment_data/file/67470/libya-isrt-June2011.pdf

"Italy to Train Thousands of Libyan Soldiers, Says Prime Minister Zaydan," *BBC Monitoring Middle East*, July 4, 2013.

Kadlec, Amanda, "A Stable Transition in Tripoli, Actually," *The Daily Star*, February 21, 2012.

Khalil, Ezzeldeen, "Minding the Militias," *Janes Intelligence Review*, January 17, 2013.

Khan, Mohsin, and Karim Mezran, "The Libyan Economy After the Revolution: Still No Clear Vision," Atlantic Council Issue Brief, August 28, 2013. As of September 23, 2013:
http://www.atlanticcouncil.org/publications/issue-briefs/the-libyan-economy-after-the-revolution-still-no-clear-vision

Kilcullen, David, *The Accidental Guerilla*, New York: Oxford University Press, 2009.

Kirkpatrick, David D., "In Turnaround, Libyan Militias Want to Keep Their Arms," *International Herald Tribune*, November 3, 2011, p. 5.

————, "Libya Democracy Clashes With Fervor for Jihad," *The New York Times*, June 23, 2012a, p. A1.

————, "Suspect in Libya Attack, in Plain Sight, Scoffs at U.S.," *The New York Times*, October 18, 2012b, p. A1

————, "A Deadly Mix in Benghazi," *The New York Times*, December 28, 2013. As of December 31, 2013:
http://www.nytimes.com/projects/2013/benghazi/#/?chapt=0

Krauss, Clifford, "In Libya, Unrest Brings Oil Industry to Standstill," *The New York Times*, September 12, 2013. As of September 20, 2013:
http://www.nytimes.com/2013/09/13/world/africa/in-libya-unrest-brings-oil-industry-to-standstill.html?_r=0

Lacher, Wolfram, "Fault Lines of the Revolution: Political Actors, Camps, and Conflicts in the New Libya," SWP Research Paper, May 2013.

Lederach, John Paul, *Building Peace: Sustainable Reconciliation in Divided Societies*, Washington, D.C.: U.S. Institute of Peace Press, 1997.

Lekic, Slobodan, "NATO Urges Libyan Authorities to Seize Arms Caches," Associated Press, October 3, 2011.

"Lībīya Tahzhur al-Fawā'id al-Masrafīya [Libya Prohibits Bank Interest]," *Al-jazeera.net*, January 7, 2013.

"Libya Tribal Leaders Break Away from Interim Government," Associated Press, March 6, 2012.

"Libya: Uneasy Calm in Sebha After Clashes," *IRIN*, May 14, 2012. As of October 18, 2013:
http://www.irinnews.org/report/95446/libya-uneasy-calm-in-sebha-after-clashes

"Libyan Official Says 50 Killed, 150 Injured in Sebha Clashes," *BBC Monitoring Middle East*, March 28, 2012.

"Libyan Premier Discusses Security, Border Issues, Cooperation with US," *BBC Monitoring Middle East*, September 26, 2013.

Loyd, Anthony, "Al-Qa'ida Eyes Gaddafi's Missiles and Uranium," *The Australian*, October 23, 2013.

Makan, Ajay, "Libya and International Oil Groups Pay the Price for Unrest," *Financial Times*, September 16, 2011.

Mandraud, Isabelle, "Poussée de fièvre à Benghazi contre le journal satirique [High Fever in Benghazi Against the Satirical Newspaper]," *Le Monde*, September 20, 2012.

Martin, Felix, and Gerald Knaus, "Travails of the European Raj," *Journal of Democracy*, Vol. 14, No. 3, 2003.

Mason, T. David, Mehmet Gurses, Patrick T. Brandt, and Jason Michael Quinn, "When Civil Wars Recur: Conditions for Durable Peace After Civil Wars," *International Studies Perspectives*, Vol. 12, 2011, pp. 171–189.

McQuinn, Brian, "Armed Groups in Libya: Typology and Roles," *Small Arms Survey*, No. 18, June 2012a. As of October 18, 2013: http://www.smallarmssurvey.org/fileadmin/docs/H-Research_Notes/SAS-Research-Note-18.pdf

———, *After the Fall: Libya's Evolving Armed Groups*, Geneva, Switzerland: Small Arms Survey, October 2012b.

Meo, Nick, and Hassan Morajea, "Militia Chaos in Bani Walid Raises Danger of Civil War in Post-Gaddafi Libya," *The Telegraph*, January 28, 2012. As of October 18, 2013: http://www.telegraph.co.uk/news/worldnews/africaandindianocean/libya/9046372/Militia-chaos-in-Bani-Walid-raises-danger-of-civil-war-in-post-Gaddafi-Libya.html

Mezran, Karim, and Fadel Lamen, "Security Challenges to Libya's Quest for Democracy," *Atlantic Council Issue Brief*, September 2012.

Mezran, Karim, and Duncan Pickard, "Libya's Constitutional Process: Moving Forward?" The Atlantic Council, April 13, 2013.

Miller, Laurel, ed., *Framing the State in Times of Transition: Case Studies in Constitution Making*, Washington, D.C.: U.S. Institute of Peace, 2010.

"Ministries of Interior and Defence Move to Stamp Out Renegade Militias," *Libya Herald*, March 19, 2013. As of October 18, 2013: http://www.libyaherald.com/2013/03/19/ministry-of-interior-and-defense-form-joint-security-force/#axzz2i5ZbUiCu

Mohamed, Essam, and Jamel Arfaoui, "Libya: Ultimatum Issued to Militias," *Maghrebia*, June 13, 2013. As of October 18, 2013: http://allafrica.com/stories/201306140650.html

Mustafa, Abdul-Jalil, "Libyan Police Trainees Arrested in Jordan After Riots and Arson," *Libya Herald*, July 11, 2012.

Narten, Jens, "Dilemmas of Promoting 'Local Ownership': The Case of Postwar Kosovo," in Roland Paris and Timothy D. Sisk, eds., *The Dilemmas of Statebuilding: Confronting the Contradictions of Postwar Peace Operations,* New York: Routledge, 2009.

National Center for the Support of Decision-Making, "Al-Sīra al-Dhātīya lil Wuzarā' al-dhīna Qadamahum Ra'īs al-Hukūma al-Muntakhab al-Sayyed 'Ali Zeidan [The Biographies of the Ministers Presented by the Elected Prime Minister of the Government Mr. Ali Zeidan]," undated. As of April 1, 2013: http://www.npdc.gov.ly/index.php?option=com_content&view=article&id=187:2012-10-30-11-53-39&catid=10:2012-08-02-22-31-25&Itemid=16

National Democratic Institute, "Believing in Democracy: Public Opinion Survey in Libya," August 2013a.

———, "Seeking Security: Public Opinion Survey in Libya," November 2013b.

Natsios, Andrew S., "The Nine Principles of Reconstruction and Development," *Parameters*, Autumn 2005.

Nisman, Daniel, "The Jihadist Gateway to Africa," *Wall Street Journal*, January 21, 2013.

"Oil Strikes Cost Libya $130 Million per Day," UPI, September 13, 2011. As of September 20, 2013: http://www.upi.com/Business_News/Energy-Resources/2013/09/13/Oil-strikes-cost-Libya-130-million-per-day/UPI-47741379076857/

Organization for the Prohibition of Chemical Weapons, "Libya: Facts and Figures," undated. As of January 20, 2014: http://www.opcw.org/the-opcw-and-libya/libya-facts-and-figures/

Osborne, Peter, "With Gaddafi Gone, Who Will Run the New Libya?" *The Telegraph*, October 20, 2011.

Pack, Jason, ed., *The 2011 Libyan Uprisings and the Struggle for the Post Qadhafi Future*, New York: Palgrave, 2013.

Pargeter, Allison, *Libya: The Rise and Fall of Qaddafi*, New Haven, Conn.: Yale University Press, 2012.

———, "Islamist Militant Groups in Post-Qadhafi Libya, " *CTC Sentinel*, Vol. 6, No. 2, February 2013. As of October 18, 2013: http://www.ctc.usma.edu/posts/february-2013

Paris, Roland, *At War's End: Building Peace After Civil Conflict,* Cambridge: Cambridge University Press, 2004.

———, "Saving Liberal Peacebuilding," *Review of International Studies*, Vol. 36, 2010, pp. 337–365.

Perito, Robert M., and Alison Laporte-Oshiro, "Libya: Security Sector Reconstruction," *United States Institute of Peace*, July 5, 2012.

Quinlivin, James T., "Force Requirements in Stability Operations," *Parameters*, Winter 1995, pp. 59–69

Quinn, J. Michael, T. David Mason, and Mehmet Gurses, "Sustaining the Peace: Determinants of Civil War Recurrence," *International Interactions*, Vol. 33, No. 2, 2007, pp. 167–193.

Raleigh, Clionadh, Andrew Linke, Håvard Hegre, and Joakim Karlsen, "Introducing ACLED-Armed Conflict Location and Event Data," *Journal of Peace Research*, Vol. 47, No. 5, 2010, pp. 1–10.

Robertson, Nic, Paul Cruickshank, and Tim Lister, "Growing Concern over Jihadist 'Safe Haven' in Eastern Libya," CNN.com, May 15, 2012. As of October 18, 2013:
http://security.blogs.cnn.com/2012/05/15/
growing-concern-over-jihadist-safe-haven-in-eastern-libya/

Ruhayem, Ahmed, "Federalists Celebrate Return of NOC to Benghazi," *Libya Herald*, June 7, 2013. As of September 20, 2013:
http://www.libyaherald.com/2013/06/07/
federalists-celebrates-return-of-noc-to-benghazi/#axzz2fSvIH7HH

"Sensitive Weapons Stolen from US Special Forces in Libya May Have Fallen in Wrong Hands," *Tripolipost.com*, September 15, 2013. As of February 14, 2014:
http://www.tripolipost.com/articledetail.asp?c=1&i=10641

Schmitt, Eric, "U.S. to Help Create an Elite Libyan Force to Combat Islamic Extremists," *The New York Times,* October 15, 2012.

Snyder, Jack, and Robert Jervis, "Civil War and the Security Dilemma," in Barbara F. Walter and Jack Snyder, eds., *Civil Wars, Insecurity, and Intervention,* New York: Columbia University Press, September 2009.

Spencer, Richard, "France Supplying Weapons to Libyan Rebels," *The Telegraph,* June 29, 2011.

Stack, Liam, "Pro-Government Libyan Militia Routed from a Qaddafi Bastion," *The New York Times*, January 24, 2012. As of October 18, 2013:
http://www.nytimes.com/2012/01/25/world/africa/pro-government-libyan-militia-routed-from-qaddafi-bastion.html?_r=0

Stewart, Rory, and Gerald Knaus, *Can Intervention Work?* New York: Norton, 2011.

"Thousands of Libyan Missiles from Qaddafi Era Missing in Action," *CBS News*, March 25, 2013.

"UN Envoy Says 6,400 Barrels of Yellowcake Is Stored in Libya" *BBC News*, December 10, 2013.

United Nations, *Consolidated Report of the Integrated Pre-Assessment Process for Libya Post-Conflict Planning*, Working Draft August 5, 2011.

―――, "Transnational Organized Crime in West Africa," undated. As of January 20, 2014:
http://www.unodc.org/documents/toc/Reports/TOCTAWestAfrica/West_Africa_TOC_FIREARMS.pdf

―――, "Report of the Secretary General on the United Nations Support Mission in Libya," UN Document S/201/675, August 30, 2012.

United Nations Office for the Coordination of Humanitarian Affairs, "Libya Response," Situation Report No. 65, October 31, 2011. As of October 9, 2013:
http://libya.humanitarianresponse.info/sites/default/files/111031_OCHA_SituationReportNo.65_LibyaResponse.pdf

United Nations Security Council, "6698th Meeting Transcript," New York, UN Document S/PV/6698, December 22, 2011. As of October 11, 2013:
http://www.un.org/en/ga/search/view_doc.asp?symbol=S/PV.6698

―――, "Report of the Secretary General on the United National Support Mission in Libya," UN Document S/2011/727, November 22, 2011. As of October 9, 2013:
http://daccess-dds-ny.un.org/doc/UNDOC/GEN/N11/592/47/PDF/N1159247.pdf?OpenElement

―――, "Ian Martin's Report at the 6728th Session of the UN Security Council on February 29, 2012," UN Document S/PV.6728, February 29, 2012.

―――, "The Situation in Libya," Security Council report S/PV.6639, October 26, 2011. As of October 9, 2013:
http://www.securitycouncilreport.org/atf/cf/%7B65BFCF9B-6D27-4E9C-8CD3-CF6E4FF96FF9%7D/Libya%20S%20PV%206639.pdf

"Unity Under Strain," *Africa Confidential*, Vol. 53, No. 25, December 14, 2012. As of October 18, 2013:
http://www.africa-confidential.com/article-preview/id/4721/Unity_under_strain

U.S. Army, *Field Manual 3.0: Operations*, Washington, D.C.: Headquarters, Department of the Army, February 2008.

U.S. Embassy, Tripoli, "Ambassador's Eid Message," August 5, 2013.

U.S. Energy Information Administration, "Libya: Analysis," June 2012. As of October 22, 2012:
http://www.eia.gov/countries/country-data.cfm?fips=LY

―――, "International Energy Statistics," data files on global oil production, 2013. As of February 11, 2014:
http://www.eia.gov/cfapps/ipdbproject/iedindex3.cfm?tid=5&pid=53&aid=1&cid=regions,&syid=2009&eyid=2013&unit=TBPD

Vandewalle, Dirk, *History of Modern Libya*, New York: Cambridge University Press, 2012.

Wahab, Ashraf Abdul, and Nigel Ash, "Weaponry Plundering Prompts U.S. Training Withdrawal," *Libya Herald*, September 17, 2013.

Watts, Stephen, Caroline Baxter, Molly Dunigan, and Christopher Rizzi, *The Uses and Limits of Small-Scale Military Interventions*, Santa Monica, Calif.: RAND Corporation, MG-1226-RC, 2012. As of January 20, 2014: http://www.rand.org/pubs/monographs/MG1226.html

Wehrey, Frederic, "Libya's Militia Menace: The Challenge After the Elections," *Foreign Affairs,* July 12, 2012a. As of October 18, 2013: http://www.foreignaffairs.com/articles/137776/frederic-wehrey/libyas-militia-menace

———, "The Struggle for Security in Eastern Libya," Carnegie Endowment, September 19, 2012b. As of October 18, 2013: http://carnegieendowment.org/2012/09/19/struggle-for-security-in-eastern-libya/dvct

Wehrey, Frederic, and Peter Cole, *Building Libya's Security Sector*, Washington, D.C.: Carnegie Endowment for International Peace, August 2013.

Zargoun, Taha, and Oliver Holmes, "Libyan Official in Talks with Unruly Town," *Washington Post*, January 26, 2012.

Zway, Suliman Ali, and Kareem Fahim, "Libyan Militia Fires on Protesters," *The New York Times*, June 10, 2013, p. 8.